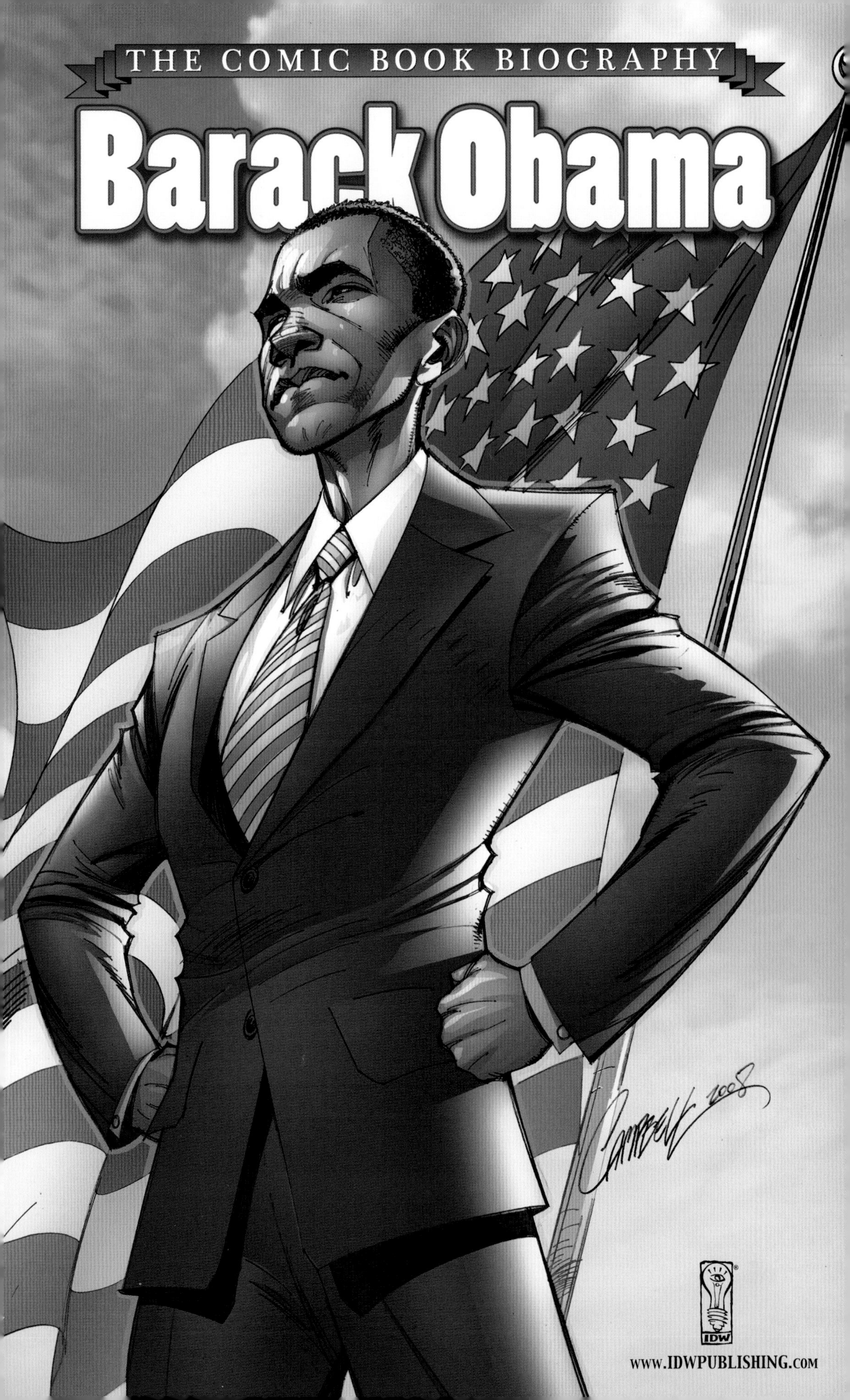
THE COMIC BOOK BIOGRAPHY
Barack Obama
Campbell 2008
IDW
www.IDWPUBLISHING.com

Written by Jeff Mariotte

Art by Tom Morgan

Color by Len O'Grady & John Hunt

Letters by Robbie Robbins & Neil Uyetake

Cover by J. Scott Campbell

Cover Color by Edgar Delgado

Original Edits by Scott Dunbier

Collection Edits by Justin Eisinger

Editorial Assistance by Mariah Huehner

Collection Design by Chris Mowry

ABC News, Anchorage Daily News, Associated Press, BBC, Bloomberg.com, Boston Globe, CBS News, Chicago Magazine, Chicago Sun-Times, Chicago Tribune, Christian Science Monitor, Cleveland Plain Dealer, CNN, Denver Post, Factcheck.org, Foxnews.com, Gallup.com, Guardian, Huffingtonpost.com, International Herald Tribune, London Times, Los Angeles Times, Mediamatters.org, Miami Herald, MSNBC.com, MTV, NBC, New Republic, Newsweek, Newsday, New York Daily News, New York Post, New York Times Magazine, NFL.com, NPR, Politico.com, Pollingreport.com, Reuters, Rolling Stone, San Francisco Chronicle, Scranton Times-Tribune, Senate.gov, Time, United Press International, USA Today, Wall Street Journal, Washington Post, Washington Times, Whitehouse.gov

Conversations portrayed on pages 4, 5, 7, 8, 10, 12, 14 are quoted from *Dreams From My Father* by Barack Obama

Conversations portrayed on pages 19, 21, 23 are quoted from *The Audacity of Hope* by Barack Obama

Operations: Ted Adams, Chief Executive Officer • Greg Goldstein, Chief Operating Officer • Matthew Ruzicka, CPA, Chief Financial Officer • Alan Payne, VP of Sales • Lorelei Bunjes, Dir. of Digital Services • AnnaMaria White, Marketing & PR Manager • Marci Hubbard, Executive Assistant • Alonzo Simon, Shipping Manager • Angela Loggins, Staff Accountant • Editorial: Chris Ryall, Publisher/Editor-in-Chief • Scott Dunbier, Editor, Special Projects • Andy Schmidt, Senior Editor • Justin Eisinger, Editor • Kris Oprisko, Editor/Foreign Lic. • Denton J. Tipton, Editor • Tom Waltz, Editor • Mariah Huehner, Associate Editor • Carlos Guzman, Editorial Assistant • Design: Robbie Robbins, EVP/Sr. Graphic Artist • Neil Uyetake, Art Director • Chris Mowry, Graphic Artist • Amauri Osorio, Graphic Artist • Gilberto Lazcano, Production Assistant

www.idwpublishing.com

ISBN: 978-1-60010-530-2
12 11 10 09   1 2 3 4

PRESIDENTIAL MATERIAL

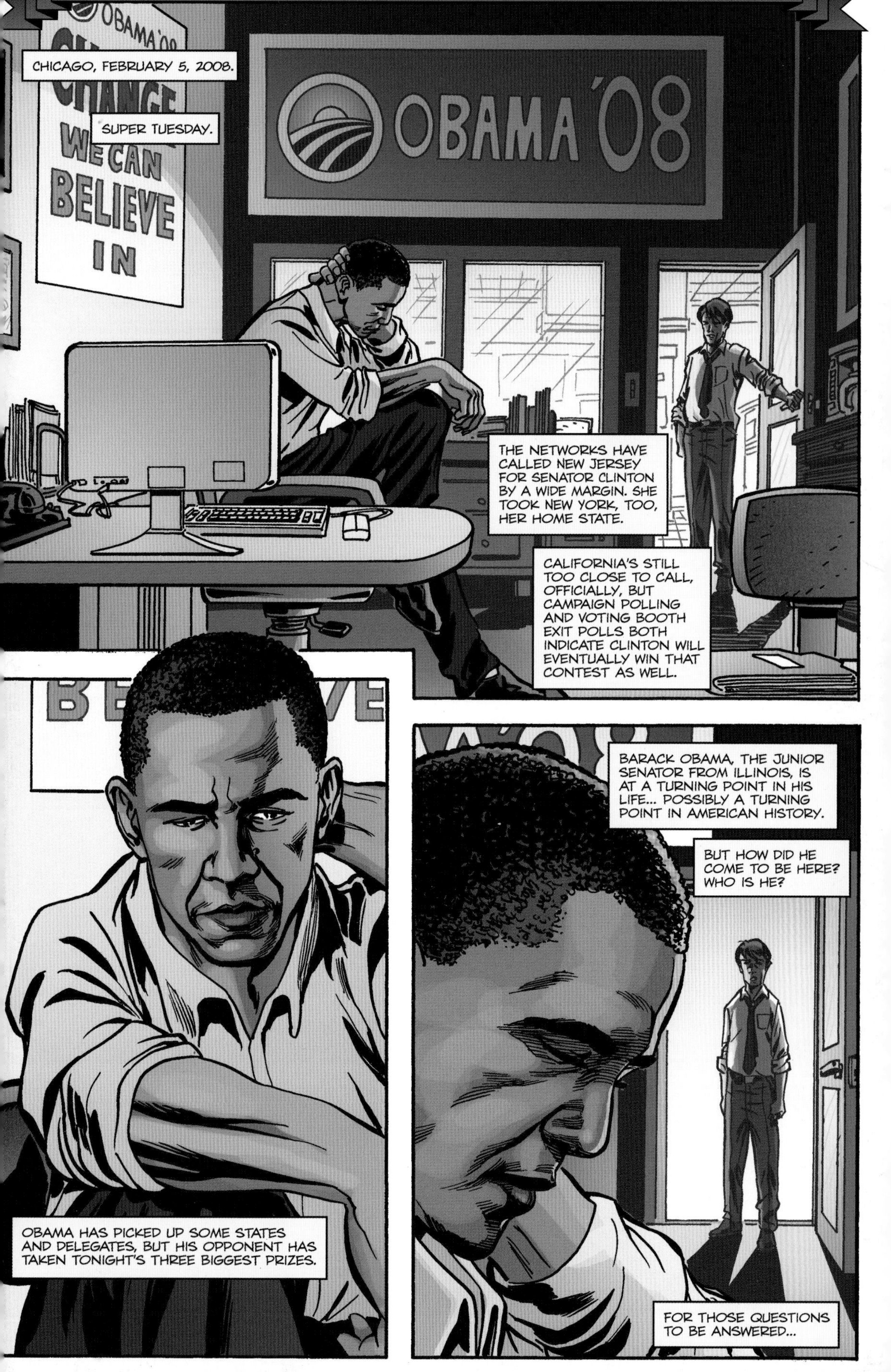
CHICAGO, FEBRUARY 5, 2008.
SUPER TUESDAY.
OBAMA '08
CHANGE WE CAN BELIEVE IN
OBAMA '08
THE NETWORKS HAVE CALLED NEW JERSEY FOR SENATOR CLINTON BY A WIDE MARGIN. SHE TOOK NEW YORK, TOO, HER HOME STATE.
CALIFORNIA'S STILL TOO CLOSE TO CALL, OFFICIALLY, BUT CAMPAIGN POLLING AND VOTING BOOTH EXIT POLLS BOTH INDICATE CLINTON WILL EVENTUALLY WIN THAT CONTEST AS WELL.
OBAMA HAS PICKED UP SOME STATES AND DELEGATES, BUT HIS OPPONENT HAS TAKEN TONIGHT'S THREE BIGGEST PRIZES.
BARACK OBAMA, THE JUNIOR SENATOR FROM ILLINOIS, IS AT A TURNING POINT IN HIS LIFE... POSSIBLY A TURNING POINT IN AMERICAN HISTORY.
BUT HOW DID HE COME TO BE HERE? WHO IS HE?
FOR THOSE QUESTIONS TO BE ANSWERED...

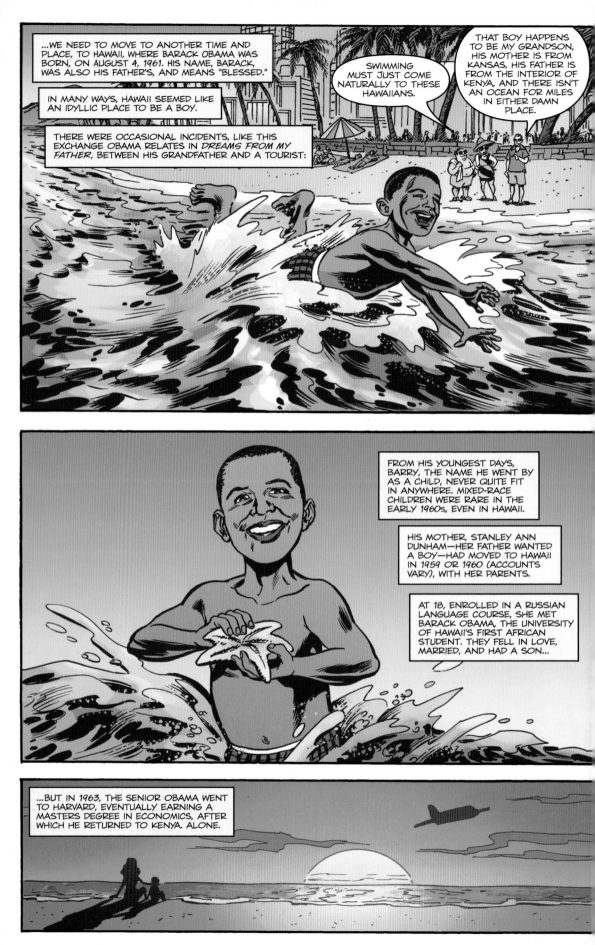

...WE NEED TO MOVE TO ANOTHER TIME AND PLACE, TO HAWAII, WHERE BARACK OBAMA WAS BORN, ON AUGUST 4, 1961. HIS NAME, BARACK, WAS ALSO HIS FATHER'S, AND MEANS "BLESSED."

IN MANY WAYS, HAWAII SEEMED LIKE AN IDYLLIC PLACE TO BE A BOY.

THERE WERE OCCASIONAL INCIDENTS, LIKE THIS EXCHANGE OBAMA RELATES IN *DREAMS FROM MY FATHER*, BETWEEN HIS GRANDFATHER AND A TOURIST:

SWIMMING MUST JUST COME NATURALLY TO THESE HAWAIIANS.

THAT BOY HAPPENS TO BE MY GRANDSON, HIS MOTHER IS FROM KANSAS, HIS FATHER IS FROM THE INTERIOR OF KENYA, AND THERE ISN'T AN OCEAN FOR MILES IN EITHER DAMN PLACE.

FROM HIS YOUNGEST DAYS, BARRY, THE NAME HE WENT BY AS A CHILD, NEVER QUITE FIT IN ANYWHERE. MIXED-RACE CHILDREN WERE RARE IN THE EARLY 1960s, EVEN IN HAWAII.

HIS MOTHER, STANLEY ANN DUNHAM—HER FATHER WANTED A BOY—HAD MOVED TO HAWAII IN 1959 OR 1960 (ACCOUNTS VARY), WITH HER PARENTS.

AT 18, ENROLLED IN A RUSSIAN LANGUAGE COURSE, SHE MET BARACK OBAMA, THE UNIVERSITY OF HAWAII'S FIRST AFRICAN STUDENT. THEY FELL IN LOVE, MARRIED, AND HAD A SON...

...BUT IN 1963, THE SENIOR OBAMA WENT TO HARVARD, EVENTUALLY EARNING A MASTERS DEGREE IN ECONOMICS, AFTER WHICH HE RETURNED TO KENYA. ALONE.

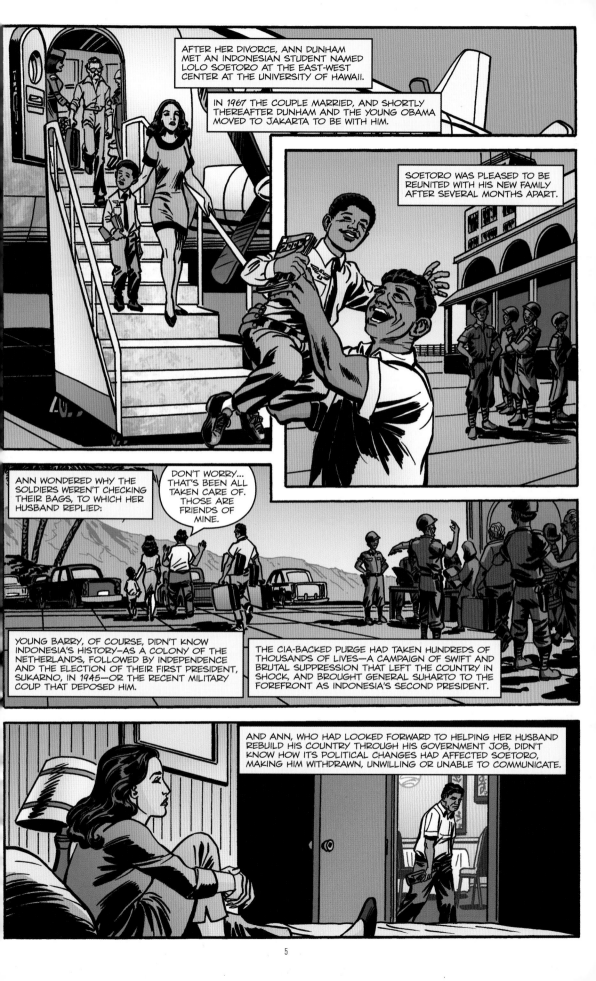

AFTER HER DIVORCE, ANN DUNHAM MET AN INDONESIAN STUDENT NAMED LOLO SOETORO AT THE EAST-WEST CENTER AT THE UNIVERSITY OF HAWAII.

IN 1967 THE COUPLE MARRIED, AND SHORTLY THEREAFTER DUNHAM AND THE YOUNG OBAMA MOVED TO JAKARTA TO BE WITH HIM.

SOETORO WAS PLEASED TO BE REUNITED WITH HIS NEW FAMILY AFTER SEVERAL MONTHS APART.

ANN WONDERED WHY THE SOLDIERS WEREN'T CHECKING THEIR BAGS, TO WHICH HER HUSBAND REPLIED:

DON'T WORRY... THAT'S BEEN ALL TAKEN CARE OF. THOSE ARE FRIENDS OF MINE.

YOUNG BARRY, OF COURSE, DIDN'T KNOW INDONESIA'S HISTORY—AS A COLONY OF THE NETHERLANDS, FOLLOWED BY INDEPENDENCE AND THE ELECTION OF THEIR FIRST PRESIDENT, SUKARNO, IN 1945—OR THE RECENT MILITARY COUP THAT DEPOSED HIM.

THE CIA-BACKED PURGE HAD TAKEN HUNDREDS OF THOUSANDS OF LIVES—A CAMPAIGN OF SWIFT AND BRUTAL SUPPRESSION THAT LEFT THE COUNTRY IN SHOCK, AND BROUGHT GENERAL SUHARTO TO THE FOREFRONT AS INDONESIA'S SECOND PRESIDENT.

AND ANN, WHO HAD LOOKED FORWARD TO HELPING HER HUSBAND REBUILD HIS COUNTRY THROUGH HIS GOVERNMENT JOB, DIDN'T KNOW HOW ITS POLITICAL CHANGES HAD AFFECTED SOETORO, MAKING HIM WITHDRAWN, UNWILLING OR UNABLE TO COMMUNICATE.

LATER, WORKING FOR AN AMERICAN OIL COMPANY, SOETORO'S FORTUNES IMPROVED. HE WAS ABLE TO AFFORD A NICER HOUSE, A CAR, TO SIGN FOR MEALS AT THE COMPANY CLUB.

SOME OF HER HUSBAND'S PRACTICES DISTURBED ANN, LIKE HIDING THE REFRIGERATOR WHEN TAX OFFICIALS CAME SO THEY WOULDN'T SEE HOW WELL HE WAS DOING.

INDONESIA WAS AN IMPOVERISHED COUNTRY, AND HE DIDN'T WANT PEOPLE TO KNOW HE MADE ENOUGH MONEY TO AFFORD SUCH LUXURIES.

HE INSISTED THAT EVERYONE EXPECTED IT, EVEN THE TAX OFFICIALS. BUT THAT DIDN'T MAKE IT RIGHT TO HIS WIFE.

SHE WANTED HER SON TO KNOW THAT HONESTY WAS IMPORTANT. HIS FATHER WAS AN HONEST MAN. HONESTY, FAIRNESS, STRAIGHT TALK, INDEPENDENT JUDGMENT—THESE WERE CRUCIAL TRAITS FOR A MAN TO HAVE.

LITTLE MAYA, OBAMA'S BABY SISTER BORN IN 1970, NEEDED TO GROW UP WITH AN HONORABLE BIG BROTHER.

YOUNG BARRY'S EDUCATION CAME FROM EVERY DIRECTION AT ONCE—FROM 1967 TO 1970 HE ATTENDED FRANSISKUS STRADA ASISIA, A CATHOLIC SCHOOL, FOLLOWED BY TWO YEARS AT PUBLIC ELEMENTARY SCHOOL MENTENG NO. 1, A PREDOMINANTLY MUSLIM SCHOOL, AS WELL AS CORRESPONDENCE COURSES, THE STREETS, HIS MOTHER'S LESSONS AND THE BOOKS AND RECORDS ABOUT THE CIVIL RIGHTS MOVEMENT SHE GAVE HIM.

ONCE AGAIN, HE WAS UNIQUE, DIFFERENT FROM THOSE AROUND HIM.

MARTIN LUTHER KING JR. SPEAKS!

HIS MOTHER TRIED TO TEACH HIM TO EMBRACE THAT DIFFERENCE, AS WELL AS THE AFRICAN SIDE OF HIS HERITAGE, EVEN THOUGH HE HAD NO ROLE MODEL FOR THAT.

OBAMA'S MOTHER DECIDED HE WOULD BE BETTER OFF IN AN AMERICAN SCHOOL, SO SHE SENT HIM BACK TO HAWAII TO LIVE WITH HER PARENTS, STANLEY AND MADELYN DUNHAM, WHOM HE CALLED TOOT AND GRAMPS.

HE APPLIED TO, AND WAS ACCEPTED BY, THE PRESTIGIOUS PUNAHOU ACADEMY.

OBAMA, IN *DREAMS FROM MY FATHER*, RECALLED HIS FIRST DAY OF SCHOOL:

HI THERE. THIS HERE'S BARRY. I'M BARRY'S GRANDFATHER. YOU CAN CALL ME GRAMPS. BARRY'S NEW.

ME TOO.

YOUR GRANDFATHER'S FUNNY.

YEAH. HE IS.

INSIDE THE CLASSROOM, THERE WERE SNICKERS WHEN THE TEACHER CALLED OUT THE NAME BARACK OBAMA.

7

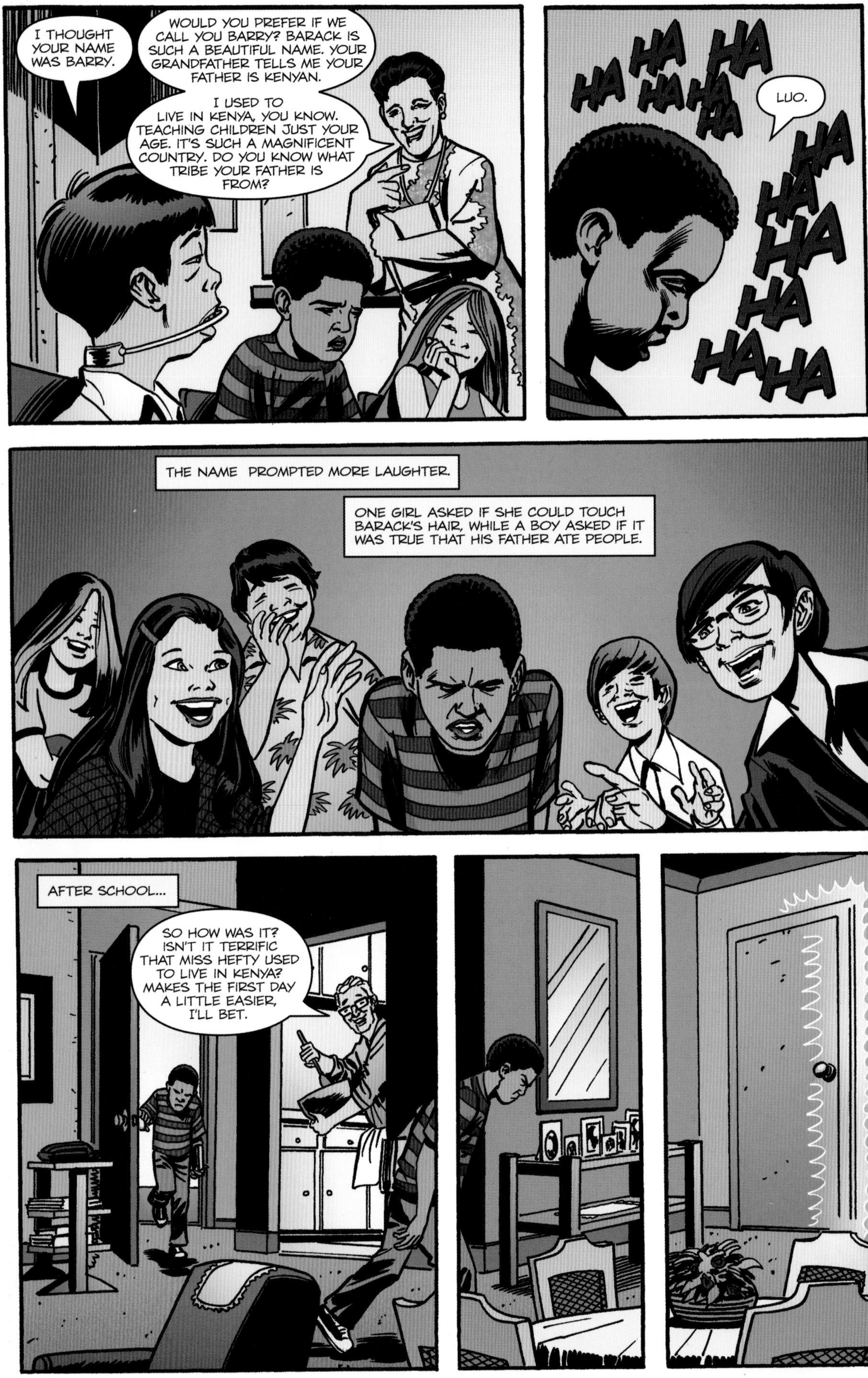
I THOUGHT YOUR NAME WAS BARRY.
WOULD YOU PREFER IF WE CALL YOU BARRY? BARACK IS SUCH A BEAUTIFUL NAME. YOUR GRANDFATHER TELLS ME YOUR FATHER IS KENYAN.
I USED TO LIVE IN KENYA, YOU KNOW. TEACHING CHILDREN JUST YOUR AGE. IT'S SUCH A MAGNIFICENT COUNTRY. DO YOU KNOW WHAT TRIBE YOUR FATHER IS FROM?
LUO.
HA HA HA HA HA HA HA
HA HA HA HA HA HA HA
THE NAME PROMPTED MORE LAUGHTER.
ONE GIRL ASKED IF SHE COULD TOUCH BARACK'S HAIR, WHILE A BOY ASKED IF IT WAS TRUE THAT HIS FATHER ATE PEOPLE.
AFTER SCHOOL...
SO HOW WAS IT? ISN'T IT TERRIFIC THAT MISS HEFTY USED TO LIVE IN KENYA? MAKES THE FIRST DAY A LITTLE EASIER, I'LL BET.

SEPARATED FROM SOETORO, OBAMA'S MOTHER AND SISTER RETURNED TO HAWAII IN 1972, WHERE HIS MOTHER PURSUED A MASTER'S DEGREE. OBAMA, 11, LIVED WITH THEM FOR THREE YEARS, UNTIL SHE RETURNED TO INDONESIA TO DO ANTHROPOLOGICAL FIELDWORK. SHE WOULD EARN A PHD IN ANTHROPOLOGY IN 1992.

CHOOSING TO STAY BEHIND, OBAMA AGAIN LIVED WITH TOOT AND GRAMPS. HE SEARCHED FOR HIS IDENTITY, TRYING TO LEARN WHAT IT MEANT TO BE A BLACK MAN IN AN AMERICA CHANGING AS FAST AS HE WAS.

EVEN ON HIS HIGH SCHOOL BASKETBALL TEAM, AT PUNAHOU ACADEMY, HE FELT HE WAS IN THE WHITE MAN'S WORLD. BUT PLAYING WITH OLDER FRIENDS ON THE NEARBY UNIVERSITY COURTS, HE WAS FREE TO BE HIMSELF.

HE SOUGHT OUT THE COMPANY OF OTHER BLACK MEN, READ ELLISON, BALDWIN, HUGHES, WRIGHT, DUBOIS, AND MALCOLM X, AND TRIED TO FIGURE OUT WHERE HE BELONGED. HE WAS EXPERIMENTING WITH TOBACCO, ALCOHOL, POT, AND COCAINE.

"THINGS HAD GOTTEN COMPLICATED," OBAMA LATER WROTE, REFERRING TO THAT PERIOD IN HIS LIFE.

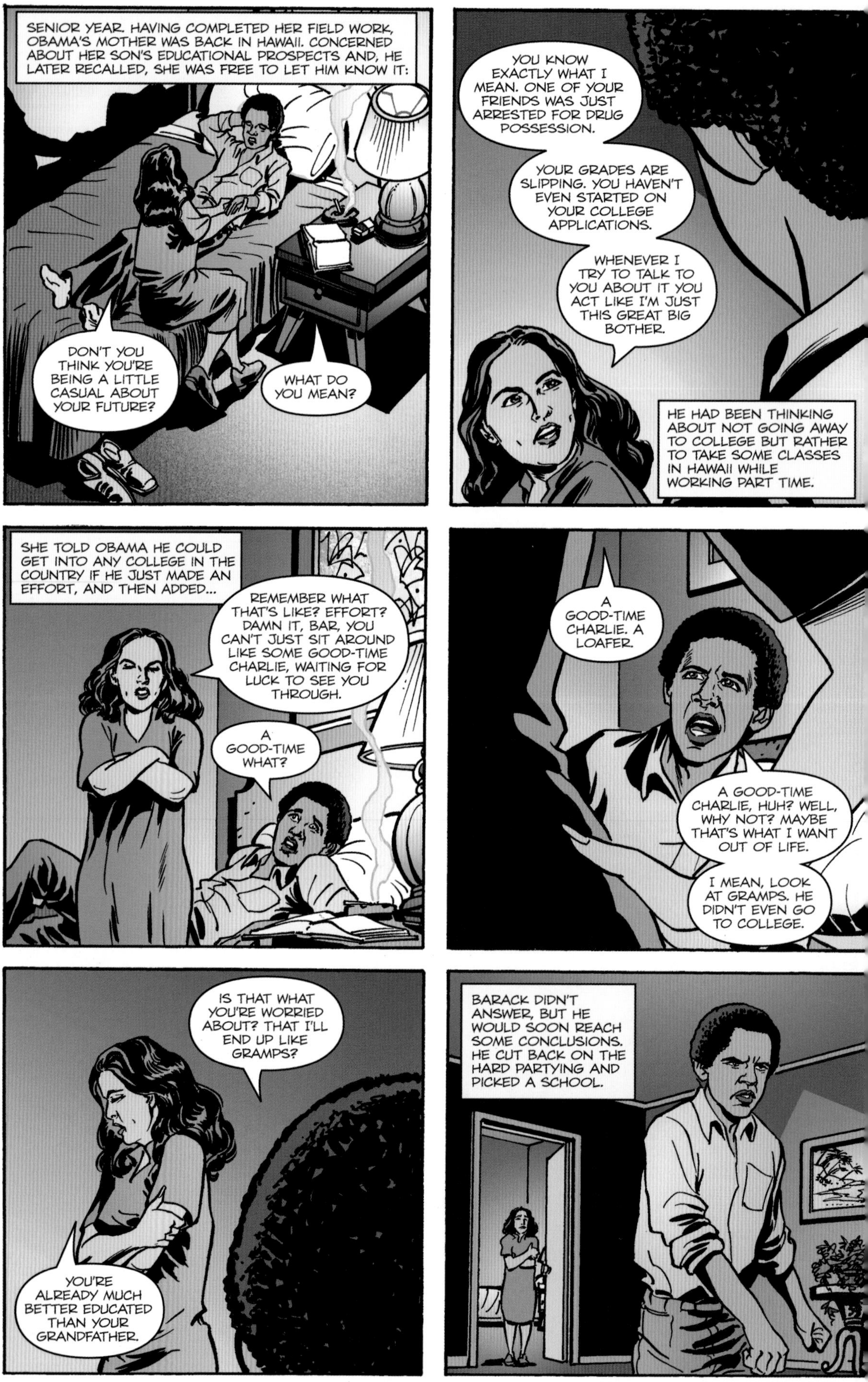
SENIOR YEAR. HAVING COMPLETED HER FIELD WORK, OBAMA'S MOTHER WAS BACK IN HAWAII. CONCERNED ABOUT HER SON'S EDUCATIONAL PROSPECTS AND, HE LATER RECALLED, SHE WAS FREE TO LET HIM KNOW IT:
DON'T YOU THINK YOU'RE BEING A LITTLE CASUAL ABOUT YOUR FUTURE?
WHAT DO YOU MEAN?
YOU KNOW EXACTLY WHAT I MEAN. ONE OF YOUR FRIENDS WAS JUST ARRESTED FOR DRUG POSSESSION.
YOUR GRADES ARE SLIPPING. YOU HAVEN'T EVEN STARTED ON YOUR COLLEGE APPLICATIONS.
WHENEVER I TRY TO TALK TO YOU ABOUT IT YOU ACT LIKE I'M JUST THIS GREAT BIG BOTHER.
HE HAD BEEN THINKING ABOUT NOT GOING AWAY TO COLLEGE BUT RATHER TO TAKE SOME CLASSES IN HAWAII WHILE WORKING PART TIME.
SHE TOLD OBAMA HE COULD GET INTO ANY COLLEGE IN THE COUNTRY IF HE JUST MADE AN EFFORT, AND THEN ADDED...
REMEMBER WHAT THAT'S LIKE? EFFORT? DAMN IT, BAR, YOU CAN'T JUST SIT AROUND LIKE SOME GOOD-TIME CHARLIE, WAITING FOR LUCK TO SEE YOU THROUGH.
A GOOD-TIME WHAT?
A GOOD-TIME CHARLIE. A LOAFER.
A GOOD-TIME CHARLIE, HUH? WELL, WHY NOT? MAYBE THAT'S WHAT I WANT OUT OF LIFE.
I MEAN, LOOK AT GRAMPS. HE DIDN'T EVEN GO TO COLLEGE.
IS THAT WHAT YOU'RE WORRIED ABOUT? THAT I'LL END UP LIKE GRAMPS?
YOU'RE ALREADY MUCH BETTER EDUCATED THAN YOUR GRANDFATHER.
BARACK DIDN'T ANSWER, BUT HE WOULD SOON REACH SOME CONCLUSIONS. HE CUT BACK ON THE HARD PARTYING AND PICKED A SCHOOL.

OCCIDENTAL COLLEGE, LOS ANGELES. SOME OF HIS NEW FRIENDS PERSUADED HIM TO RETURN TO HIS GIVEN NAME–BARACK, NOT BARRY. DURING CHRISTMAS BREAK IN 1980, BACK IN HAWAII, HE TOLD HIS FAMILY. IT WAS A DECISION HE NEVER WENT BACK ON.

THERE HE BECAME FRIENDS WITH OTHER MULTIRACIAL STUDENTS... SOME OF WHOM RESENTED BEING CALLED BLACK AND DIDN'T WANT TO HAVE TO CHOOSE ONE PART OF THEIR RACIAL HERITAGE OVER OTHERS SIMPLY BECAUSE OF THEIR SKIN COLOR.

ONE FRIEND, OBAMA RECALLED, DID NOT BELIEVE WHITE PEOPLE WANTED HER TO PICK A SINGLE RACE AND LIVE WITH THAT AS A FINAL DECISION, BUT SHE FELT BLACK PEOPLE PUSHED HER IN THAT DIRECTION.

BARACK LATER WROTE, "I CHOSE MY FRIENDS CAREFULLY. THE MORE POLITICALLY ACTIVE BLACK STUDENTS. THE FOREIGN STUDENTS. THE CHICANOS.

"THE MARXIST PROFESSORS AND STRUCTURAL FEMINISTS AND PUNK-ROCK PERFORMANCE POETS.

"WHEN WE GROUND OUT OUR CIGARETTES IN THE HALLWAY CARPET OR SET OUR STEREOS SO LOUD THAT THE WALLS BEGAN TO SHAKE, WE WERE RESISTING BOURGEOIS SOCIETY'S STIFLING CONSTRAINTS.

"WE SMOKED CIGARETTES AND WORE LEATHER JACKETS. AT NIGHT, IN THE DORMS, WE DISCUSSED NEOCOLONIALISM, FRANTZ FANON, EUROCENTRISM, AND PATRIARCHY.

"WE WEREN'T INDIFFERENT OR CARELESS OR INSECURE. WE WERE ALIENATED."

ON THE THEORY THAT COLUMBIA UNIVERSITY WOULD HAVE A LARGER BLACK POPULATION—OR FAILING THAT, NEW YORK WOULD HAVE BLACK NEIGHBORHOODS—BARACK TRANSFERRED THERE.

BECOMING A COMMUNITY ORGANIZER, A DREAM FROM HIS COLLEGE DAYS, WAS SLIPPING FARTHER AWAY BY THE DAY.

THEN ONE DAY HE RECEIVED A PHONE CALL FROM SOMEONE NAMED AUMA.

BZZT

AUMA WAS AN AFRICAN HALF-SISTER OBAMA HAD NEVER MET. SHE HAD LEFT KENYA TO STUDY IN GERMANY. NOW SHE WAS COMING TO THE U.S. WITH FRIENDS AND WANTED TO VISIT BARACK IN NEW YORK.

OF COURSE. YOU CAN STAY WITH ME, I CAN'T WAIT.

HE SPENT WEEKS PREPARING FOR COMPANY.

TWO DAYS BEFORE HER ARRIVAL, THOUGH, HE GOT ANOTHER CALL.

I CAN'T COME AFTER ALL. ONE OF OUR BROTHERS, DAVID... HE'S BEEN KILLED. IN A MOTORCYCLE ACCIDENT.

OH, BARACK. WHY DO THESE THINGS HAPPEN TO US?

BARACK TOOK THE REST OF THE DAY OFF AND WALKED THE STREETS OF MANHATTAN, THINKING ABOUT FAMILY HE HAD NEVER KNOWN, ABOUT HIS LATE FATHER, WHO HAD DIED IN 1982. WHO HE HAD ONLY MET ONCE SINCE HIS SECOND YEAR.

THINKING ABOUT THE NECESSITY OF DOING WHAT HIS HEART TOLD HIM HE SHOULD, WHILE HE STILL HAD TIME.

WITHIN MONTHS, HE HAD RESIGNED HIS CORPORATE JOB AND BEGAN LOOKING FOR WORK AS A COMMUNITY ORGANIZER.

IN 1985 OBAMA MOVED TO CHICAGO.

EXIT

HIRED BY THE DEVELOPING COMMUNITIES PROJECT, HE WENT TO WORK ON THE CITY'S IMPOVERISHED SOUTH SIDE. NOT ALL HIS EFFORTS PANNED OUT OR WERE MET WITH MUCH FANFARE.

BUT SOME DID—MORE AND MORE AS THE MONTHS PASSED HE BECAME BETTER KNOWN IN CHICAGO'S ACTIVIST COMMUNITY.

HE LEARNED TO LISTEN TO PEOPLE, TO DRAW OUT THEIR STORIES ABOUT THEMSELVES AND THEIR LIVES—AND IN TURN, TO TELL STORIES OF HIS OWN PERSONAL EXPERIENCES AS WELL AS HIS HOPES AND EXPECTATIONS FOR THE FUTURE.

THESE STORIES HELPED HIM FIND THE SENSE OF PURPOSE HE HAD BEEN SEEKING FOR SO LONG.

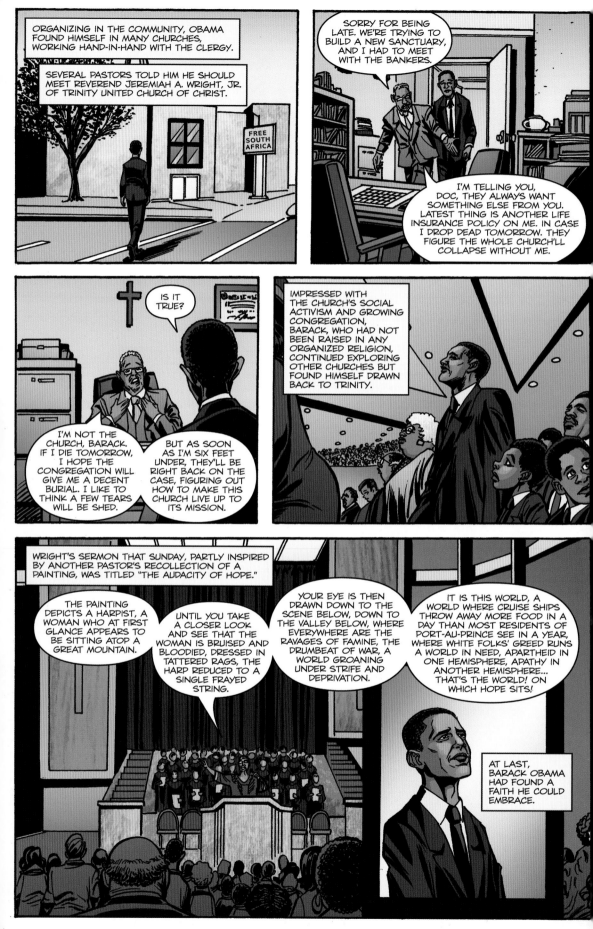

ORGANIZING IN THE COMMUNITY, OBAMA FOUND HIMSELF IN MANY CHURCHES, WORKING HAND-IN-HAND WITH THE CLERGY.

SEVERAL PASTORS TOLD HIM HE SHOULD MEET REVEREND JEREMIAH A. WRIGHT, JR. OF TRINITY UNITED CHURCH OF CHRIST.

FREE SOUTH AFRICA

SORRY FOR BEING LATE. WE'RE TRYING TO BUILD A NEW SANCTUARY, AND I HAD TO MEET WITH THE BANKERS.

I'M TELLING YOU, DOC, THEY ALWAYS WANT SOMETHING ELSE FROM YOU. LATEST THING IS ANOTHER LIFE INSURANCE POLICY ON ME. IN CASE I DROP DEAD TOMORROW. THEY FIGURE THE WHOLE CHURCH'LL COLLAPSE WITHOUT ME.

IS IT TRUE?

I'M NOT THE CHURCH, BARACK. IF I DIE TOMORROW, I HOPE THE CONGREGATION WILL GIVE ME A DECENT BURIAL. I LIKE TO THINK A FEW TEARS WILL BE SHED.

BUT AS SOON AS I'M SIX FEET UNDER, THEY'LL BE RIGHT BACK ON THE CASE, FIGURING OUT HOW TO MAKE THIS CHURCH LIVE UP TO ITS MISSION.

IMPRESSED WITH THE CHURCH'S SOCIAL ACTIVISM AND GROWING CONGREGATION, BARACK, WHO HAD NOT BEEN RAISED IN ANY ORGANIZED RELIGION, CONTINUED EXPLORING OTHER CHURCHES BUT FOUND HIMSELF DRAWN BACK TO TRINITY.

WRIGHT'S SERMON THAT SUNDAY, PARTLY INSPIRED BY ANOTHER PASTOR'S RECOLLECTION OF A PAINTING, WAS TITLED "THE AUDACITY OF HOPE."

THE PAINTING DEPICTS A HARPIST, A WOMAN WHO AT FIRST GLANCE APPEARS TO BE SITTING ATOP A GREAT MOUNTAIN.

UNTIL YOU TAKE A CLOSER LOOK AND SEE THAT THE WOMAN IS BRUISED AND BLOODIED, DRESSED IN TATTERED RAGS, THE HARP REDUCED TO A SINGLE FRAYED STRING.

YOUR EYE IS THEN DRAWN DOWN TO THE SCENE BELOW, DOWN TO THE VALLEY BELOW, WHERE EVERYWHERE ARE THE RAVAGES OF FAMINE, THE DRUMBEAT OF WAR, A WORLD GROANING UNDER STRIFE AND DEPRIVATION.

IT IS THIS WORLD, A WORLD WHERE CRUISE SHIPS THROW AWAY MORE FOOD IN A DAY THAN MOST RESIDENTS OF PORT-AU-PRINCE SEE IN A YEAR, WHERE WHITE FOLKS' GREED RUNS A WORLD IN NEED, APARTHEID IN ONE HEMISPHERE, APATHY IN ANOTHER HEMISPHERE... THAT'S THE WORLD! ON WHICH HOPE SITS!

AT LAST, BARACK OBAMA HAD FOUND A FAITH HE COULD EMBRACE.

BEFORE ENTERING HARVARD LAW SCHOOL, OBAMA VISITED HIS ANCESTRAL HOME IN KENYA.

HIS HALF-SISTER AUMA HAD FINALLY VISITED HIM IN CHICAGO, AND THAT VISIT CONVINCED HIM HE NEEDED TO MAKE THE JOURNEY TO KENYA TO MEET THE REST OF HIS FAMILY.

TO SEE THE PLACE THAT HAD SHAPED HIS FATHER.

OBAMA'S STEP-GRANDMOTHER, WHO HE CALLED GRANNY, RELATED STORIES OF HIS GRANDFATHER'S LIFE, AND HIS FATHER'S— HEADSTRONG MEN MAKING THEIR WAY IN AN AFRICA UNDER WHITE COLONIAL RULE, FORCED INTO THE AFFAIRS OF THE 20TH CENTURY BY WAR AND COMMERCE, BUT TRYING TO CLING TO THEIR TRADITIONAL WAYS.

GRANNY STILL HAD THE REGISTER THAT OBAMA'S GRANDFATHER USED TO RECORD ALL HIS DOMESTIC SERVANT JOBS, AND LETTERS HIS FATHER HAD WRITTEN TO UNIVERSITIES ALL OVER THE UNITED STATES—THE LETTERS THAT EVENTUALLY GAINED HIM ADMITTANCE TO THE UNIVERSITY OF HAWAII.

DOMESTIC SERVANTS POCKET REGISTRY

OBAMA RECOGNIZED HIS LEGACY IN THE STORIES AND ARTIFACTS OF THESE MEN. THE THINGS THEY HAD PASSED DOWN.

HE LATER WROTE, "I REALIZED THAT WHO I WAS, WHAT I CARED ABOUT, WAS NO LONGER JUST A MATTER OF INTELLECT OR OBLIGATION, NO LONGER A CONSTRUCT OF WORDS.

"I SAW THAT MY LIFE IN AMERICA—THE BLACK LIFE, THE WHITE LIFE, THE SENSE OF ABANDONMENT I'D FELT AS A BOY, THE FRUSTRATION AND HOPE I'D WITNESSED IN CHICAGO—ALL OF IT WAS CONNECTED WITH THIS SMALL PLOT OF EARTH AN OCEAN AWAY, CONNECTED BY MORE THAN THE ACCIDENT OF A NAME OR THE COLOR OF MY SKIN.

"THE PAIN I FELT WAS MY FATHER'S PAIN. MY QUESTIONS WERE MY BROTHERS' QUESTIONS. THEIR STRUGGLE, MY BIRTHRIGHT."

BACK IN THE STATES, AFTER THE PIVOTAL KENYA TRIP, BARACK OBAMA ATTENDED HARVARD LAW SCHOOL.

ALTHOUGH HE OFTEN FOUND THE LAW DRY AND DISSATISFYING, REFLECTING DECISIONS THAT HAD MORE TO DO WITH GREED OR CONVENIENCE THAN COMPASSION OR TRUTH, HE EXCELLED AT IT.

RENOWNED CONSTITUTIONAL LAW PROFESSOR LAURENCE TRIBE, FOR WHOM OBAMA SERVED AS A RESEARCH ASSISTANT, CALLED HIM "THE MOST ALL-AROUND IMPRESSIVE STUDENT I HAD SEEN IN DECADES."

IN 1990, BARACK BECAME THE FIRST AFRICAN-AMERICAN PRESIDENT OF THE HARVARD LAW REVIEW IN THAT PRESTIGIOUS INSTITUTION'S LONG HISTORY.

BEFORE GRADUATING MAGNA CUM LAUDE, HE HAD ALREADY RECEIVED A CONTRACT TO WRITE HIS MEMOIR, *DREAMS FROM MY FATHER*, AND BECOME ONE OF THE MOST PROMINENT LAW STUDENTS IN THE COUNTRY.

BUT CHICAGO BECKONED. WITH MORE THAN 600 OFFERS BEFORE GRADUATION, HE COULD HAVE WORKED FOR ALMOST ANY LAW FIRM IN THE NATION, BUT HE WANTED TO RETURN TO HIS ADOPTED CITY AND A CAREER IN PUBLIC-INTEREST LAW.

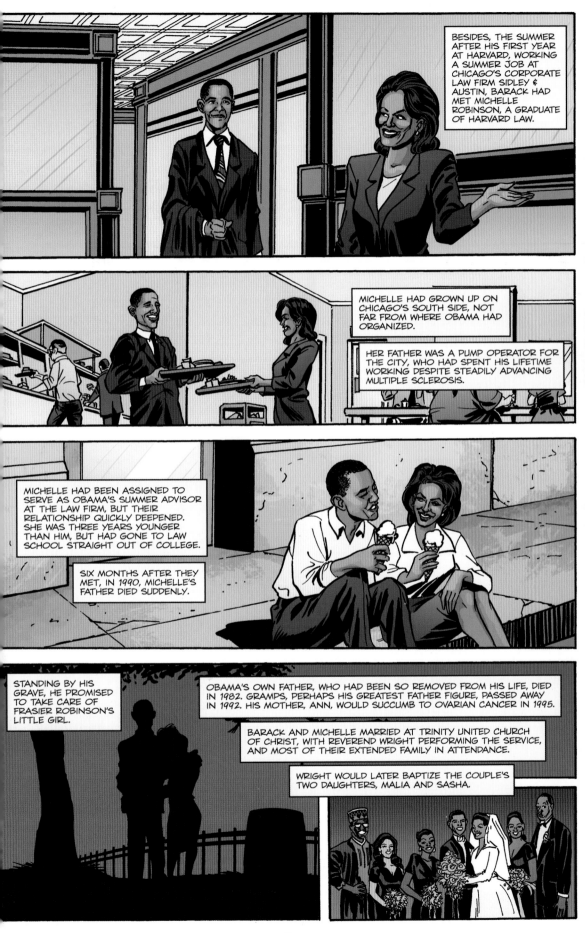

BESIDES, THE SUMMER AFTER HIS FIRST YEAR AT HARVARD, WORKING A SUMMER JOB AT CHICAGO'S CORPORATE LAW FIRM SIDLEY & AUSTIN, BARACK HAD MET MICHELLE ROBINSON, A GRADUATE OF HARVARD LAW.

MICHELLE HAD GROWN UP ON CHICAGO'S SOUTH SIDE, NOT FAR FROM WHERE OBAMA HAD ORGANIZED.

HER FATHER WAS A PUMP OPERATOR FOR THE CITY, WHO HAD SPENT HIS LIFETIME WORKING DESPITE STEADILY ADVANCING MULTIPLE SCLEROSIS.

MICHELLE HAD BEEN ASSIGNED TO SERVE AS OBAMA'S SUMMER ADVISOR AT THE LAW FIRM, BUT THEIR RELATIONSHIP QUICKLY DEEPENED. SHE WAS THREE YEARS YOUNGER THAN HIM, BUT HAD GONE TO LAW SCHOOL STRAIGHT OUT OF COLLEGE.

SIX MONTHS AFTER THEY MET, IN 1990, MICHELLE'S FATHER DIED SUDDENLY.

STANDING BY HIS GRAVE, HE PROMISED TO TAKE CARE OF FRASIER ROBINSON'S LITTLE GIRL.

OBAMA'S OWN FATHER, WHO HAD BEEN SO REMOVED FROM HIS LIFE, DIED IN 1982. GRAMPS, PERHAPS HIS GREATEST FATHER FIGURE, PASSED AWAY IN 1992. HIS MOTHER, ANN, WOULD SUCCUMB TO OVARIAN CANCER IN 1995.

BARACK AND MICHELLE MARRIED AT TRINITY UNITED CHURCH OF CHRIST, WITH REVEREND WRIGHT PERFORMING THE SERVICE, AND MOST OF THEIR EXTENDED FAMILY IN ATTENDANCE.

WRIGHT WOULD LATER BAPTIZE THE COUPLE'S TWO DAUGHTERS, MALIA AND SASHA.

IN CHICAGO, MARRIED AND PAYING OFF STUDENT LOANS, OBAMA WORKED AS AN ASSOCIATE ATTORNEY FOR THE LAW FIRM MINER BARNHILL & GALLAND, AND TAUGHT CONSTITUTIONAL LAW AT THE UNIVERSITY OF CHICAGO LAW SCHOOL.

MICHELLE WORKED AT CHICAGO'S DEPARTMENT OF PLANNING AND THEN RAN THE LOCAL BRANCH OF PUBLIC ALLIES, A NATIONAL SERVICE PROGRAM.

BY 1996, HOWEVER, HE HAD MADE THE DIFFICULT DECISION TO CAMPAIGN FOR POLITICAL OFFICE, RUNNING FOR A SEAT IN THE ILLINOIS SENATE. THE LEGISLATURE WAS DOMINATED BY REPUBLICANS, AND HE RAN AS A DEMOCRAT FROM THE 13TH DISTRICT.

IN TRADITIONAL CHICAGO STYLE, THE CANDIDATE PLAYED HARDBALL POLITICS, USING TECHNICALITIES OF THE RULES TO KNOCK POTENTIAL OPPONENTS OUT OF THE RACE BY CHALLENGING THEIR BALLOT PETITIONS—EMPLOYING THE STRICTEST INTERPRETATION OF THE LAW TO BENEFIT HIS CAMPAIGN.

HE WON BY A LARGE MARGIN, AND WHEN HE WENT TO SPRINGFIELD IN JANUARY 1997, HE QUICKLY ESTABLISHED A REPUTATION AS A STATE SENATOR ABLE TO WORK ACROSS THE AISLE.

WORKING WITH SENATORS OF BOTH PARTIES, HE HELPED CRAFT AMBITIOUS CAMPAIGN FINANCE REFORM LEGISLATION THAT MADE HIS STATE ONE OF THE NATION'S BEST IN TERMS OF CAMPAIGN FINANCE DISCLOSURE.

OBAMA SPEARHEADED A BILL REQUIRING VIDEOTAPED HOMICIDE INTERROGATIONS AND CONFESSIONS, AND ANOTHER MONITORING RACIAL PROFILING IN TRAFFIC STOPS.

IN ADDITION TO WORKING HARD, HE PLAYED HARD, PLAYING POKER IN THE EVENINGS WITH LEGISLATORS OF EVERY PARTY AND POLITICAL CREED.

IN 2000, OBAMA SUFFERED HIS ONLY POLITICAL LOSS SO FAR, WHICH HE TERMED A "DRUBBING," WHEN HE RAN FOR A SEAT IN THE U.S. HOUSE OF REPRESENTATIVES AGAINST INCUMBENT BOBBY RUSH, A FORMER MEMBER OF THE BLACK PANTHERS.

WHEN THE RESULTS OF OBAMA'S INTERNAL POLLING CAME IN, RUSH'S NAME RECOGNITION WAS AT 90%. OBAMA'S WAS 11%. RUSH'S APPROVAL RATING WAS 70%, BUT OBAMA'S—AMONG PEOPLE WHO HAD HEARD OF HIM—WAS 8%.

IT WASN'T LONG BEFORE OBAMA KNEW HE WAS IN A LOSING BATTLE. BUT HE HAD TO KEEP FIGHTING TO THE END, AND IN SPITE OF A LATE SURGE, HE LOST BY 31 POINTS.

THE LOSS WAS NOT ONLY HUMILIATING, IT WAS EXPENSIVE, DEVASTATING HIS SAVINGS AND PERSONAL CREDIT.

IN HIS SECOND BOOK, *THE AUDACITY OF HOPE*, OBAMA RECOUNTED HIS TRIP TO LOS ANGELES FOR THE 2000 DEMOCRATIC NATIONAL CONVENTION...

I'M SORRY, MR. OBAMA, BUT YOUR CARD'S BEEN REJECTED.

THAT CAN'T BE RIGHT. CAN YOU TRY AGAIN?

I TRIED TWICE, SIR. MAYBE YOU SHOULD CALL AMERICAN EXPRESS.

AN AMERICAN EXPRESS SUPERVISOR EVENTUALLY APPROVED THE TRANSACTION. ONCE HE FINALLY GOT TO THE CONVENTION THINGS WENT FURTHER DOWNHILL.

OBAMA HAD NO OFFICIAL PRESENCE THERE, NOT EVEN AS A DELEGATE, SO HE COULDN'T GET A FLOOR PASS.

HE WATCHED SOME SPEECHES ON TV SCREENS AT THE STAPLES CENTER AND THEN FLEW HOME AFTER A COUPLE OF DAYS.

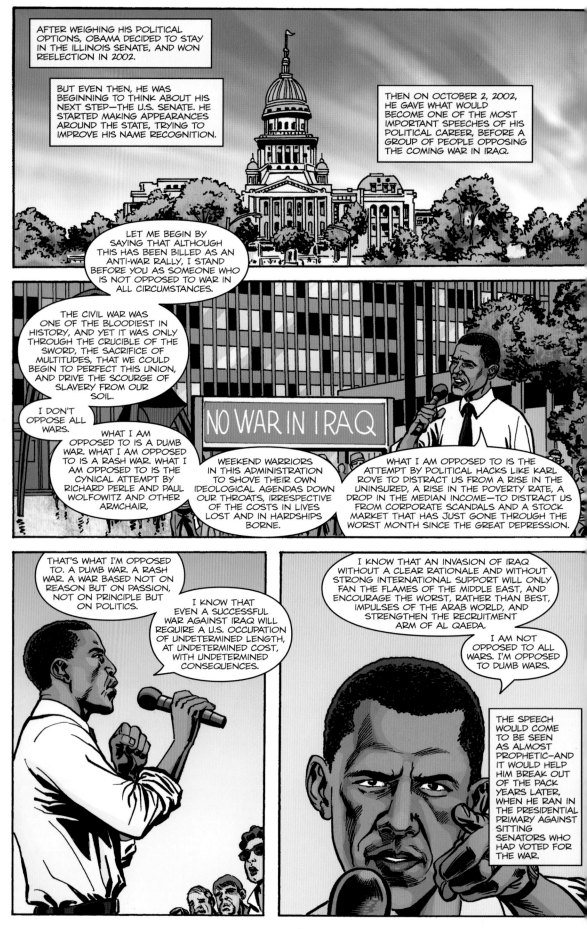

AFTER WEIGHING HIS POLITICAL OPTIONS, OBAMA DECIDED TO STAY IN THE ILLINOIS SENATE, AND WON REELECTION IN 2002.

BUT EVEN THEN, HE WAS BEGINNING TO THINK ABOUT HIS NEXT STEP—THE U.S. SENATE. HE STARTED MAKING APPEARANCES AROUND THE STATE, TRYING TO IMPROVE HIS NAME RECOGNITION.

THEN ON OCTOBER 2, 2002, HE GAVE WHAT WOULD BECOME ONE OF THE MOST IMPORTANT SPEECHES OF HIS POLITICAL CAREER, BEFORE A GROUP OF PEOPLE OPPOSING THE COMING WAR IN IRAQ.

LET ME BEGIN BY SAYING THAT ALTHOUGH THIS HAS BEEN BILLED AS AN ANTI-WAR RALLY, I STAND BEFORE YOU AS SOMEONE WHO IS NOT OPPOSED TO WAR IN ALL CIRCUMSTANCES.

THE CIVIL WAR WAS ONE OF THE BLOODIEST IN HISTORY, AND YET IT WAS ONLY THROUGH THE CRUCIBLE OF THE SWORD, THE SACRIFICE OF MULTITUDES, THAT WE COULD BEGIN TO PERFECT THIS UNION, AND DRIVE THE SCOURGE OF SLAVERY FROM OUR SOIL.

I DON'T OPPOSE ALL WARS.

WHAT I AM OPPOSED TO IS A DUMB WAR. WHAT I AM OPPOSED TO IS A RASH WAR. WHAT I AM OPPOSED TO IS THE CYNICAL ATTEMPT BY RICHARD PERLE AND PAUL WOLFOWITZ AND OTHER ARMCHAIR,

NO WAR IN IRAQ

WEEKEND WARRIORS IN THIS ADMINISTRATION TO SHOVE THEIR OWN IDEOLOGICAL AGENDAS DOWN OUR THROATS, IRRESPECTIVE OF THE COSTS IN LIVES LOST AND IN HARDSHIPS BORNE.

WHAT I AM OPPOSED TO IS THE ATTEMPT BY POLITICAL HACKS LIKE KARL ROVE TO DISTRACT US FROM A RISE IN THE UNINSURED, A RISE IN THE POVERTY RATE, A DROP IN THE MEDIAN INCOME—TO DISTRACT US FROM CORPORATE SCANDALS AND A STOCK MARKET THAT HAS JUST GONE THROUGH THE WORST MONTH SINCE THE GREAT DEPRESSION.

THAT'S WHAT I'M OPPOSED TO. A DUMB WAR. A RASH WAR. A WAR BASED NOT ON REASON BUT ON PASSION, NOT ON PRINCIPLE BUT ON POLITICS.

I KNOW THAT EVEN A SUCCESSFUL WAR AGAINST IRAQ WILL REQUIRE A U.S. OCCUPATION OF UNDETERMINED LENGTH, AT UNDETERMINED COST, WITH UNDETERMINED CONSEQUENCES.

I KNOW THAT AN INVASION OF IRAQ WITHOUT A CLEAR RATIONALE AND WITHOUT STRONG INTERNATIONAL SUPPORT WILL ONLY FAN THE FLAMES OF THE MIDDLE EAST, AND ENCOURAGE THE WORST, RATHER THAN BEST, IMPULSES OF THE ARAB WORLD, AND STRENGTHEN THE RECRUITMENT ARM OF AL QAEDA.

I AM NOT OPPOSED TO ALL WARS. I'M OPPOSED TO DUMB WARS.

THE SPEECH WOULD COME TO BE SEEN AS ALMOST PROPHETIC—AND IT WOULD HELP HIM BREAK OUT OF THE PACK YEARS LATER, WHEN HE RAN IN THE PRESIDENTIAL PRIMARY AGAINST SITTING SENATORS WHO HAD VOTED FOR THE WAR.

MICHELLE WASN'T CONVINCED THAT POLITICS WAS A PROFESSION FOR HONORABLE PEOPLE. SHE AGREED TO A SENATE RUN, THOUGH, WHICH WOULD BE OBAMA'S LAST HURRAH IF HE DIDN'T WIN.

HE APPLIED THE LESSONS OF 2000. HE WORKED HARD, AND HE GOT LUCKY, CATCHING BREAKS THAT HAD FALLEN THE OTHER WAY IN HIS CONGRESSIONAL BID.

HIS BIGGEST BREAK WAS WHEN HIS ORIGINAL REPUBLICAN OPPONENT, JACK RYAN, WAS FORCED OUT BY PERSONAL SCANDAL AND THE STATE PARTY, DESPERATE, BROUGHT IN ALAN KEYES, WHO HAD NEVER LIVED IN ILLINOIS AND HAD NEVER WON AN ELECTION.

WE GOT OUR OWN HARVARD-EDUCATED CONSERVATIVE BLACK GUY TO GO UP AGAINST THE HARVARD-EDUCATED LIBERAL BLACK GUY. HE MAY NOT WIN, BUT AT LEAST HE CAN KNOCK THAT HALO OFF YOUR HEAD.

IN ANOTHER BREAK, HE WAS INVITED TO PROVIDE THE KEYNOTE ADDRESS FOR THE 2004 DEMOCRATIC NATIONAL CONVENTION NOMINATING JOHN KERRY.

GIVEN HIS ONLY PREVIOUS EXPERIENCE AT THE PARTY'S CONVENTION, IN 2000, HE APPROACHED IT WITH SOME ANXIETY.

THIS TIME, EVERYTHING HAD TO BE RIGHT.

AND EVERYTHING WAS RIGHT. WITHIN MINUTES AFTER THE 17-MINUTE SPEECH BEGAN, PEOPLE EVERYWHERE—IN THE BOSTON HALL AND WATCHING ON PRIME-TIME TV—WERE PAYING ATTENTION TO THE RELATIVELY UNKNOWN SENATORIAL CANDIDATE FROM ILLINOIS.

I STAND HERE KNOWING THAT MY STORY IS PART OF THE LARGER AMERICAN STORY, THAT I OWE A DEBT TO ALL OF THOSE WHO CAME BEFORE ME, AND THAT, IN NO OTHER COUNTRY ON EARTH, IS MY STORY EVEN POSSIBLE.

TONIGHT, WE GATHER TO AFFIRM THE GREATNESS OF OUR NATION NOT BECAUSE OF THE HEIGHT OF OUR SKYSCRAPERS, OR THE POWER OF OUR MILITARY, OR THE SIZE OF OUR ECONOMY.

OUR PRIDE IS BASED ON A VERY SIMPLE PREMISE, SUMMED UP IN A DECLARATION MADE OVER TWO HUNDRED YEARS AGO, "WE HOLD THESE TRUTHS TO BE SELF-EVIDENT, THAT ALL MEN ARE CREATED EQUAL.

"THAT THEY ARE ENDOWED BY THEIR CREATOR WITH CERTAIN INALIENABLE RIGHTS. THAT AMONG THESE ARE LIFE, LIBERTY AND THE PURSUIT OF HAPPINESS."

NOW EVEN AS WE SPEAK, THERE ARE THOSE WHO ARE PREPARING TO DIVIDE US, THE SPIN MASTERS AND NEGATIVE AD PEDDLERS WHO EMBRACE THE POLITICS OF ANYTHING GOES.

WELL, I SAY TO THEM TONIGHT, THERE'S NOT A LIBERAL AMERICA AND A CONSERVATIVE AMERICA— THERE'S THE UNITED STATES OF AMERICA. THERE'S NOT A BLACK AMERICA AND WHITE AMERICA AND LATINO AMERICA AND ASIAN AMERICA—THERE'S THE UNITED STATES OF AMERICA.

THE PUNDITS LIKE TO SLICE-AND-DICE OUR COUNTRY INTO RED STATES AND BLUE STATES; RED STATES FOR REPUBLICANS, BLUE STATES FOR DEMOCRATS. BUT I'VE GOT NEWS FOR THEM, TOO.

WE WORSHIP AN AWESOME GOD IN THE BLUE STATES, AND WE DON'T LIKE FEDERAL AGENTS POKING AROUND OUR LIBRARIES IN THE RED STATES. WE COACH LITTLE LEAGUE IN THE BLUE STATES AND, YES, WE'VE GOT SOME GAY FRIENDS IN THE RED STATES.

THERE ARE PATRIOTS WHO OPPOSED THE WAR IN IRAQ AND THERE ARE PATRIOTS WHO SUPPORTED THE WAR IN IRAQ. WE ARE ONE PEOPLE, ALL OF US PLEDGING ALLEGIANCE TO THE STARS AND STRIPES, ALL OF US DEFENDING THE UNITED STATES OF AMERICA.

BY THE NEXT DAY, BARACK OBAMA WAS A ROCK STAR.

THE NEW YORK TIMES WROTE:

"AS HE MOVED THROUGH ROOMS AND HALLWAYS, WHISPERS FOLLOWED: PERHAPS THE MAN WHO HAD JUST PASSED WOULD BE THE FIRST BLACK PRESIDENT OF THE UNITED STATES."

BACK IN ILLINOIS, THE CROWDS FOR HIS CAMPAIGN RALLIES BALLOONED.

JOHN KERRY LOST HIS PRESIDENTIAL BID, BUT IN A BRIGHT SPOT FOR DEMOCRATS THAT NOVEMBER, BARACK OBAMA WAS SWEPT INTO THE SENATE.

HE WAS THE FIFTH AFRICAN-AMERICAN SENATOR IN U.S. HISTORY, ONLY THE THIRD TO BE POPULARLY ELECTED.

HE QUICKLY FOUND HIMSELF RECOGNIZED EVERYWHERE—EVEN AT A WHITE HOUSE EVENT...

YOU'VE GOT A BRIGHT FUTURE. VERY BRIGHT. BUT I'VE BEEN IN THIS TOWN AWHILE AND, LET ME TELL YOU, IT CAN BE TOUGH. WHEN YOU GET A LOT OF ATTENTION LIKE YOU'VE BEEN GETTING, PEOPLE START GUNNIN' FOR YA.

AND IT WON'T NECESSARILY JUST BE COMING FROM MY SIDE, YOU UNDERSTAND. FROM YOURS, TOO. EVERYBODY'LL BE WAITING FOR YOU TO SLIP, KNOW WHAT I MEAN? SO WATCH YOURSELF.

YOU KNOW, ME AND YOU GOT SOMETHING IN COMMON. WE BOTH HAD TO DEBATE ALAN KEYES. THAT GUY'S A PIECE OF WORK, ISN'T HE?

THANKS FOR THE ADVICE, MR. PRESIDENT.

AS IN ILLINOIS, HE SET RIGHT TO WORK, MASTERING THE ISSUES AND CROSSING PARTY LINES ON SIGNIFICANT LEGISLATION–WORKING WITH REPUBLICANS RICHARD LUGAR ON NUCLEAR NONPROLIFERATION, TOM COBURN ON TRANSPARENCY IN GOVERNMENT CONTRACTING, AND JOHN McCAIN ON BORDER SECURITY, IMMIGRATION AND GREENHOUSE GAS REDUCTIONS.

DURING HIS SENATE CAREER HE HAS SERVED ON COMMITTEES FOR FOREIGN RELATIONS, VETERAN'S AFFAIRS, HEALTH, EDUCATION, LABOR AND PENSIONS, AND HOMELAND SECURITY AND GOVERNMENTAL AFFAIRS.

AFTER OBAMA'S SENATE VICTORY, HIS FIRST BOOK WAS REISSUED AND HIS SECOND ONE, *THE AUDACITY OF HOPE*, CONTRACTED. THEIR FINANCIAL FORTUNES SECURE, THE OBAMAS PAID OFF STUDENT LOANS AND BOUGHT A NEW $1.6 MILLION HOUSE IN CHICAGO'S POSH KENWOOD.

BUT OBAMA'S SELF-DESCRIBED "RESTLESSNESS" PULLED HIM TOWARD A NEW GOAL, SPURRED ON BY SUPPORTERS LIKE THE ILLINOIS SENIOR SENATOR RICHARD DURBIN...

...AND ON FEBRUARY 10, 2007, BEFORE THE OLD STATE CAPITOL IN SPRINGFIELD, ILLINOIS, WHERE ABRAHAM LINCOLN MADE HIS HISTORIC "HOUSE DIVIDED" SPEECH, BARACK OBAMA ANNOUNCED HIS CAMPAIGN FOR THE PRESIDENCY OF THE UNITED STATES.

IT WAS HERE, IN SPRINGFIELD, WHERE NORTH, SOUTH, EAST AND WEST COME TOGETHER THAT I WAS REMINDED OF THE ESSENTIAL DECENCY OF THE AMERICAN PEOPLE—WHERE I CAME TO BELIEVE THAT THROUGH THIS DECENCY, WE CAN BUILD A MORE HOPEFUL AMERICA.

AND THAT IS WHY, IN THE SHADOW OF THE OLD STATE CAPITOL, WHERE LINCOLN ONCE CALLED ON A DIVIDED HOUSE TO STAND TOGETHER, WHERE COMMON HOPES AND COMMON DREAMS STILL LIVE, I STAND BEFORE YOU TODAY TO ANNOUNCE MY CANDIDACY FOR PRESIDENT OF THE UNITED STATES.

THE DEMOCRATIC FIELD WAS CROWDED, WITH FORMER FIRST LADY SENATOR HILLARY CLINTON, THE ACKNOWLEDGED FRONTRUNNER.

ALSO RUNNING WERE SENATORS JOE BIDEN, CHRIS DODD, FORMER SENATORS JOHN EDWARDS AND MIKE GRAVEL, GOVERNORS BILL RICHARDSON AND TOM VILSACK, AND CONGRESSMAN DENNIS KUCINICH.

BY THE FIRST OFFICIAL DEMOCRATIC DEBATE IN SOUTH CAROLINA, ON APRIL 26, 2007, VILSACK HAD DROPPED OUT, BUT THE REST SHARED THE STAGE.

OBAMA'S FIRST WORDS REMINDED THE AUDIENCE OF HIS EARLY OPPOSITION TO WAR IN IRAQ.

WELL, BRIAN, I AM PROUD THAT I OPPOSED THIS WAR FROM THE START, BECAUSE I THOUGHT THAT IT WOULD LEAD TO THE DISASTROUS CONDITIONS THAT WE'VE SEEN ON THE GROUND IN IRAQ.

AS CAMPAIGN MANAGER, OBAMA CHOSE LONG-TIME ALLY DAVID PLOUFFE, WITH DAVID AXELROD AS MEDIA CONSULTANT AND ROBERT GIBBS AS COMMUNICATIONS DIRECTOR.

FROM THE BEGINNING, THE CANDIDATE DECLARED THIS WOULD BE A DIFFERENT SORT OF RACE, WITH NO NEGATIVE CAMPAIGNING—ALTHOUGH AS THE RACE TIGHTENED THAT DECLARATION WOULD EVENTUALLY LOOSEN.

ADDITIONALLY, OBAMA ACCEPTED NO CONTRIBUTIONS FROM PAID LOBBYISTS OR POLITICAL ACTION COMMITTEES. IN SPITE OF THIS, HE SET NEW FUNDRAISING RECORDS, RAISING MILLIONS ONLINE AND FROM SMALL DONORS.

THROUGH THE LONG SUMMER AND FALL OF 2007, HE PRESSED HARD, BUT SO DID THE OTHER FRONTRUNNERS, CLINTON AND EDWARDS. CLINTON CONTINUED TO LEAD IN THE POLLS. OBAMA WAS HOUNDED BY CHARGES THAT HE WASN'T EXPERIENCED ENOUGH.

HE COUNTERED BY SAYING THAT EXPERIENCE AT THE NATIONAL LEVEL WAS NO SUBSTITUTE FOR GOOD JUDGMENT, OR THE KIND OF LIFE EXPERIENCE HE'D HAD AS AN ACTIVIST, ORGANIZER, AND STATE SENATOR.

HIS BIOGRAPHY WAS HIS BIGGEST ASSET.

I THINK THAT IF YOU CAN TELL PEOPLE, "WE HAVE A PRESIDENT IN THE WHITE HOUSE WHO STILL HAS A GRANDMOTHER LIVING IN A HUT ON THE SHORES OF LAKE VICTORIA AND HAS A SISTER WHO'S HALF-INDONESIAN, MARRIED TO A CHINESE-CANADIAN," THEN THEY'RE GOING TO THINK HE MAY HAVE A BETTER SENSE OF WHAT'S GOING ON IN OUR LIVES AND IN OUR COUNTRY. AND THEY'D BE RIGHT.

ONE OF THE CAMPAIGN'S BIGGEST CONTROVERSIES AROSE WHEN TWO STATES VIOLATED THE DEMOCRATIC NATIONAL COMMITTEE'S RULING THAT ONLY IOWA, NEW HAMPSHIRE, NEVADA, AND SOUTH CAROLINA COULD HOLD CONTESTS BEFORE FEBRUARY 5TH.

FLORIDA AND MICHIGAN DID SO, AND THE DEMOCRATIC CANDIDATES AGREED NOT TO CAMPAIGN IN THOSE STATES. OBAMA, BIDEN, EDWARDS, AND RICHARDSON REMOVED THEIR NAMES FROM THE MICHIGAN BALLOT.

OBAMA SCORED A DRAMATIC VICTORY IN THE IOWA CAUCUSES, WHERE RECORD-BREAKING TURNOUT HELPED HIM CARRY THE DAY.

HOPE—HOPE IS WHAT LED ME HERE TODAY. WITH A FATHER FROM KENYA, A MOTHER FROM KANSAS, AND A STORY THAT COULD ONLY HAPPEN IN THE UNITED STATES OF AMERICA.

HOPE IS THE BEDROCK OF THIS NATION. THE BELIEF THAT OUR DESTINY WILL NOT BE WRITTEN FOR US, BUT BY US, BY ALL THOSE MEN AND WOMEN WHO ARE NOT CONTENT TO SETTLE FOR THE WORLD AS IT IS, WHO HAVE THE COURAGE TO REMAKE THE WORLD AS IT SHOULD BE.

THE BIG WIN MADE HIM THE NEW FRONTRUNNER IN NEW HAMPSHIRE, BUT CLINTON CAME OUT NARROWLY AHEAD. BECAUSE OF PROPORTIONAL ALLOCATION OF DELEGATES, THE STATE WAS A VIRTUAL TIE.

CLINTON WON AGAIN IN NEVADA, BUT DELEGATE ALLOCATION RULES AWARDED MORE DELEGATES TO OBAMA. HE FOLLOWED THAT WITH A 2-TO-1 VICTORY IN SOUTH CAROLINA.

FLORIDA AND MICHIGAN CAME NEXT. HILLARY CLINTON CLAIMED VICTORY IN EACH, DESPITE THE UNRESOLVED CONTROVERSY BECAUSE BOTH STATES HAD JUMPED THE OFFICIAL PRIMARY SCHEDULE.

THEN CAME SUPER TUESDAY. 22 STATES AND AMERICAN SAMOA, ALL VOTING ON THE SAME DAY.

SOME WERE BIG ONES—NEW YORK, NEW JERSEY, AND CALIFORNIA—CRUCIAL TO ANY DEMOCRATIC VICTORY IN NOVEMBER. CLINTON WON THOSE AND 7 MORE, BUT OBAMA TOOK 13 STATES, RESULTING IN ANOTHER VIRTUAL DELEGATE TIE.

THE REST OF FEBRUARY WAS A SWEEP FOR OBAMA, WITH VICTORIES IN 10 CONTESTS IN A ROW. IN ADDITION TO A LARGE DELEGATE LEAD, HE CONTINUED TO DRAW RECORD-BREAKING CONTRIBUTIONS.

THE OTHER CANDIDATES HAD DROPPED OUT, LEAVING A HISTORIC TWO-PERSON CONTEST. EITHER THE DEMOCRATIC NOMINEE WOULD BE THE FIRST MAJOR-PARTY FEMALE CANDIDATE, OR THE FIRST AFRICAN-AMERICAN CANDIDATE. BOTH SCENARIOS HAD MILLIONS OF BACKERS, AND EMOTIONS RAN HIGH.

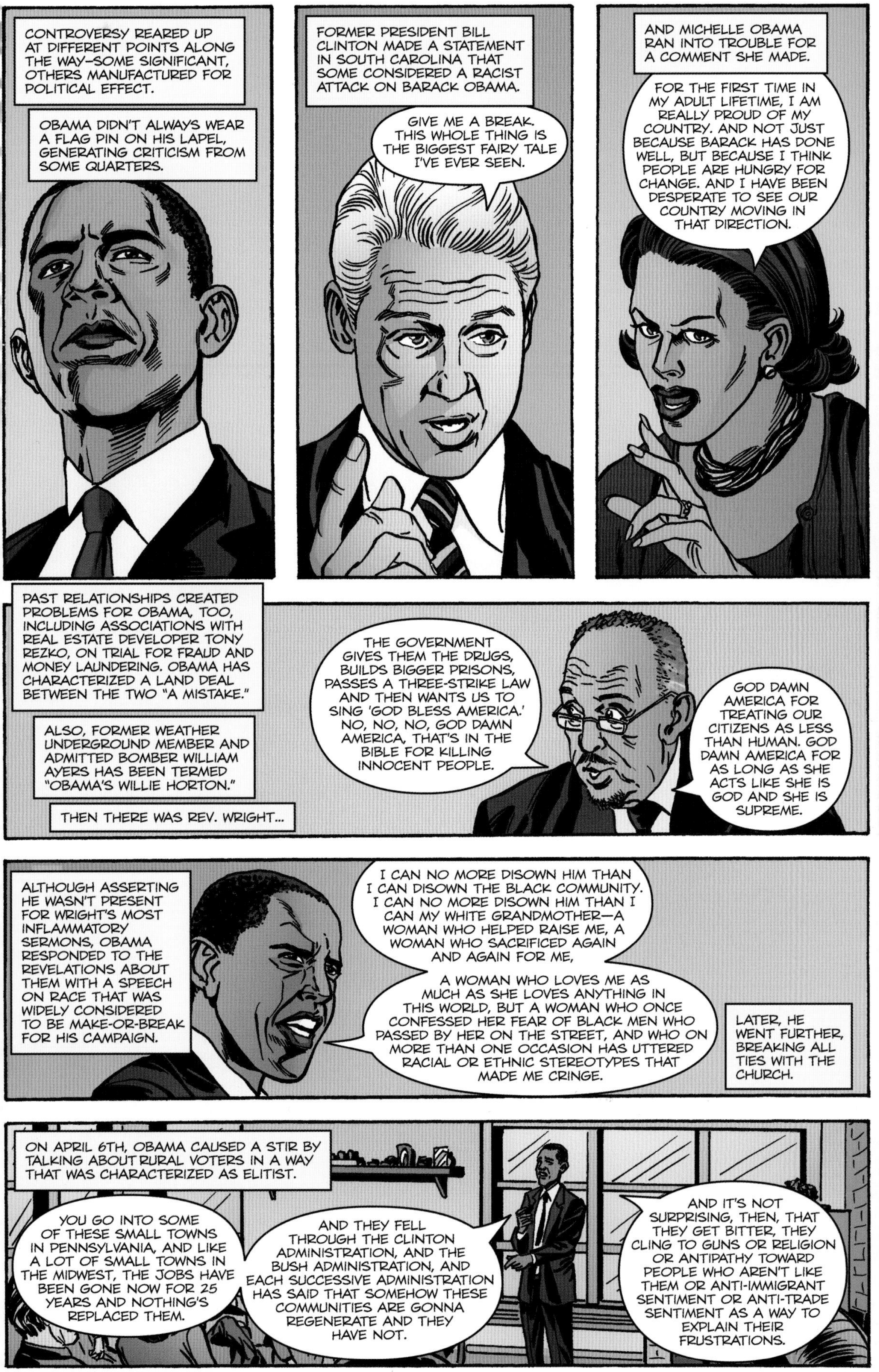

CONTROVERSY REARED UP AT DIFFERENT POINTS ALONG THE WAY—SOME SIGNIFICANT, OTHERS MANUFACTURED FOR POLITICAL EFFECT.
OBAMA DIDN'T ALWAYS WEAR A FLAG PIN ON HIS LAPEL, GENERATING CRITICISM FROM SOME QUARTERS.
FORMER PRESIDENT BILL CLINTON MADE A STATEMENT IN SOUTH CAROLINA THAT SOME CONSIDERED A RACIST ATTACK ON BARACK OBAMA.
GIVE ME A BREAK. THIS WHOLE THING IS THE BIGGEST FAIRY TALE I'VE EVER SEEN.
AND MICHELLE OBAMA RAN INTO TROUBLE FOR A COMMENT SHE MADE.
FOR THE FIRST TIME IN MY ADULT LIFETIME, I AM REALLY PROUD OF MY COUNTRY. AND NOT JUST BECAUSE BARACK HAS DONE WELL, BUT BECAUSE I THINK PEOPLE ARE HUNGRY FOR CHANGE. AND I HAVE BEEN DESPERATE TO SEE OUR COUNTRY MOVING IN THAT DIRECTION.
PAST RELATIONSHIPS CREATED PROBLEMS FOR OBAMA, TOO, INCLUDING ASSOCIATIONS WITH REAL ESTATE DEVELOPER TONY REZKO, ON TRIAL FOR FRAUD AND MONEY LAUNDERING. OBAMA HAS CHARACTERIZED A LAND DEAL BETWEEN THE TWO "A MISTAKE."
ALSO, FORMER WEATHER UNDERGROUND MEMBER AND ADMITTED BOMBER WILLIAM AYERS HAS BEEN TERMED "OBAMA'S WILLIE HORTON."
THEN THERE WAS REV. WRIGHT...
THE GOVERNMENT GIVES THEM THE DRUGS, BUILDS BIGGER PRISONS, PASSES A THREE-STRIKE LAW AND THEN WANTS US TO SING 'GOD BLESS AMERICA.' NO, NO, NO, GOD DAMN AMERICA, THAT'S IN THE BIBLE FOR KILLING INNOCENT PEOPLE.
GOD DAMN AMERICA FOR TREATING OUR CITIZENS AS LESS THAN HUMAN. GOD DAMN AMERICA FOR AS LONG AS SHE ACTS LIKE SHE IS GOD AND SHE IS SUPREME.
ALTHOUGH ASSERTING HE WASN'T PRESENT FOR WRIGHT'S MOST INFLAMMATORY SERMONS, OBAMA RESPONDED TO THE REVELATIONS ABOUT THEM WITH A SPEECH ON RACE THAT WAS WIDELY CONSIDERED TO BE MAKE-OR-BREAK FOR HIS CAMPAIGN.
I CAN NO MORE DISOWN HIM THAN I CAN DISOWN THE BLACK COMMUNITY. I CAN NO MORE DISOWN HIM THAN I CAN MY WHITE GRANDMOTHER—A WOMAN WHO HELPED RAISE ME, A WOMAN WHO SACRIFICED AGAIN AND AGAIN FOR ME,
A WOMAN WHO LOVES ME AS MUCH AS SHE LOVES ANYTHING IN THIS WORLD, BUT A WOMAN WHO ONCE CONFESSED HER FEAR OF BLACK MEN WHO PASSED BY HER ON THE STREET, AND WHO ON MORE THAN ONE OCCASION HAS UTTERED RACIAL OR ETHNIC STEREOTYPES THAT MADE ME CRINGE.
LATER, HE WENT FURTHER, BREAKING ALL TIES WITH THE CHURCH.
ON APRIL 6TH, OBAMA CAUSED A STIR BY TALKING ABOUT RURAL VOTERS IN A WAY THAT WAS CHARACTERIZED AS ELITIST.
YOU GO INTO SOME OF THESE SMALL TOWNS IN PENNSYLVANIA, AND LIKE A LOT OF SMALL TOWNS IN THE MIDWEST, THE JOBS HAVE BEEN GONE NOW FOR 25 YEARS AND NOTHING'S REPLACED THEM.
AND THEY FELL THROUGH THE CLINTON ADMINISTRATION, AND THE BUSH ADMINISTRATION, AND EACH SUCCESSIVE ADMINISTRATION HAS SAID THAT SOMEHOW THESE COMMUNITIES ARE GONNA REGENERATE AND THEY HAVE NOT.
AND IT'S NOT SURPRISING, THEN, THAT THEY GET BITTER, THEY CLING TO GUNS OR RELIGION OR ANTIPATHY TOWARD PEOPLE WHO AREN'T LIKE THEM OR ANTI-IMMIGRANT SENTIMENT OR ANTI-TRADE SENTIMENT AS A WAY TO EXPLAIN THEIR FRUSTRATIONS.

IN SPITE OF THESE SETBACKS, THE PRIMARY SEASON CONTINUED TO BE A VIRTUAL DEAD HEAT, WITH BOTH OBAMA AND HILLARY CLINTON MARKING WINS.

SOME CALLED FOR CLINTON TO DROP OUT, AS OBAMA'S LEAD GREW. BUT SHE CONTINUED WINNING CONTESTS AND STAYED IN.

IN PORTLAND, OREGON, HE DREW THE LARGEST CROWD OF THE CAMPAIGN, WHEN 75,000 PEOPLE SHOWED UP FOR A RALLY.

THE BIG WIN IN OREGON, AND DELEGATES GATHERED IN HIS LOSS IN KENTUCKY, GAVE OBAMA A VIRTUALLY INSURMOUNTABLE LEAD IN PLEDGED DELEGATES.

ON MAY 31, THE DEMOCRATIC NATIONAL COMMITTEE'S RULES COMMITTEE MET TO END THE DEBATE OVER MICHIGAN AND FLORIDA.

THEY DECIDED TO SEAT THOSE DELEGATIONS AT HALF STRENGTH, DASHING CLINTON'S HOPES AND FIRMING UP OBAMA'S LEAD.

28

THE FINAL TWO PRIMARIES, IN SOUTH DAKOTA AND MONTANA, WERE HELD ON JUNE 3.

DURING THE DAY, A SLIDE OF SUPER-DELEGATES TOWARD OBAMA GUARANTEED HIM THE MAGIC NUMBER OF 2,118 DELEGATES NEEDED FOR THE NOMINATION, AND THE TV NETWORKS ANNOUNCED HIS WIN THE MINUTE POLLS CLOSED IN MONTANA. MSNBC ANCHOR KEITH OLBERMANN REFLECTED ON THE HISTORIC EVENT.

WE HAVE HURTLED ANOTHER BARRIER THAT SO MANY COUNTRIES HAVE FAILED TO DO, AND WE HAVE FAILED TO DO SO MANY TIMES. IT IS AN EXTRAORDINARY MOMENT.

ALTHOUGH DURING A CONFERENCE CALL THAT DAY CLINTON SAID SHE WOULD BE "OPEN" TO SERVING AS OBAMA'S RUNNING MATE, WHEN CLINTON SPOKE THAT EVENING, SHE DID NOT CONCEDE THE RACE.

I WILL BE MAKING NO DECISIONS TONIGHT.

OBAMA DIDN'T NEED SENATOR CLINTON TO CONCEDE BEFORE HE CLAIMED VICTORY, THOUGH. THE MATH WAS ON HIS SIDE.

BEFORE A CAPACITY CROWD AT THE XCEL CENTER IN ST. PAUL, MINNESOTA, HE TOOK THE STAGE IN A JUBILANT MOOD.

TONIGHT, AFTER FIFTY-FOUR HARD-FOUGHT CONTESTS, OUR PRIMARY SEASON HAS FINALLY COME TO AN END. SIXTEEN MONTHS HAVE PASSED SINCE WE FIRST STOOD TOGETHER ON THE STEPS OF THE OLD STATE CAPITOL IN SPRINGFIELD, ILLINOIS.

THOUSANDS OF MILES HAVE BEEN TRAVELED. MILLIONS OF VOICES HAVE BEEN HEARD. AND BECAUSE OF WHAT YOU SAID—BECAUSE YOU DECIDED THAT CHANGE MUST COME TO WASHINGTON; BECAUSE YOU BELIEVED THAT THIS YEAR MUST BE DIFFERENT THAN ALL THE REST;

BECAUSE YOU CHOSE TO LISTEN NOT TO YOUR DOUBTS OR YOUR FEARS BUT TO YOUR GREATEST HOPES AND HIGHEST ASPIRATIONS, TONIGHT WE MARK THE END OF ONE HISTORIC JOURNEY WITH THE BEGINNING OF ANOTHER—A JOURNEY THAT WILL BRING A NEW AND BETTER DAY TO AMERICA.

TONIGHT, I CAN STAND BEFORE YOU AND SAY THAT I WILL BE THE DEMOCRATIC NOMINEE FOR PRESIDENT OF THE UNITED STATES.

CHANGE
WE CAN BELIEVE IN

WHETHER HE WINS THE PRESIDENCY OR NOT, BY BECOMING THE FIRST AFRICAN-AMERICAN CANDIDATE OF A MAJOR PARTY, WITH A GOOD SHOT AT THE WHITE HOUSE, BARACK OBAMA HAS ALREADY MADE HISTORY.

HE HAS FOUND THE PLACE HE BELONGS, THE COMMUNITY HE HAS SOUGHT FOR A LIFETIME, AND IT IS IN THE HEARTS AND MINDS OF MILLIONS OF AMERICAN VOTERS.

NEXT: THE ROAD TO THE WHITE HOUSE.

THE ROAD TO THE WHITE HOUSE

THE DEMOCRATIC NATIONAL CONVENTION.

AUGUST 25 TO 28, 2008.

UNITY IS WHAT ILLINOIS SENATOR BARACK OBAMA NEEDED MOST AT THE DEMOCRATIC NATIONAL CONVENTION—A UNIFIED DEMOCRATIC PARTY THAT COULD PUT A BRUTAL, BRUISING PRIMARY SEASON BEHIND IT.

DEMOCRATS TRADITIONALLY ARE NOT AS GOOD AT SHOWING A UNIFIED FRONT AS THEIR RIVALS IN THE REPUBLICAN PARTY.

OBAMA HAD CALMED SOME PARTY FAITHFUL BY PICKING DELAWARE SENATOR JOE BIDEN AS HIS RUNNING MATE. BIDEN WAS WORKING CLASS, TOUGH, AND HAD EXPERIENCE IN AREAS, LIKE FOREIGN POLICY, WHERE OBAMA'S WAS LIGHT.

BUT SOME OF SENATOR CLINTON'S SUPPORTERS, WHO THOUGHT SHE HAD EARNED THE VICE PRESIDENT SPOT, WERE UPSET AND THREATENED A CONVENTION FIGHT.

SO WHEN HILLARY CLINTON—OBAMA'S RIVAL IN THE CONTENTIOUS DEMOCRATIC PRIMARIES—TOOK THE STAGE AND FIRMLY ENDORSED THE ILLINOIS SENATOR, IT WAS A RELIEF TO THE OBAMA TEAM.

TODAY, AS I SUSPEND MY CAMPAIGN, I CONGRATULATE HIM ON THE VICTORY HE HAS WON AND THE EXTRAORDINARY RACE HE HAS RUN. I ENDORSE HIM AND THROW MY FULL SUPPORT BEHIND HIM.

SENATOR CLINTON MOVED TO SUSPEND THE ROLL CALL VOTE AND PRONOUNCE OBAMA THE NOMINEE BY ACCLAMATION.

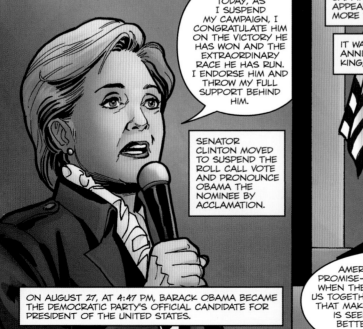

ON AUGUST 27, AT 4:47 PM, BARACK OBAMA BECAME THE DEMOCRATIC PARTY'S OFFICIAL CANDIDATE FOR PRESIDENT OF THE UNITED STATES.

CAPPING THE WEEK WAS A TRIUMPHANT APPEARANCE AT INVESCO FIELD, BEFORE MORE THAN 80,000 SUPPORTERS.

IT WAS AUGUST 28, 2008, THE 45TH ANNIVERSARY OF MARTIN LUTHER KING, JR.'S "I HAVE A DREAM" SPEECH.

IT IS THAT AMERICAN SPIRIT—THAT AMERICAN PROMISE—THAT PUSHES US FORWARD EVEN WHEN THE PATH IS UNCERTAIN; THAT BINDS US TOGETHER IN SPITE OF OUR DIFFERENCES; THAT MAKES US FIX OUR EYE NOT ON WHAT IS SEEN, BUT WHAT IS UNSEEN, THAT BETTER PLACE AROUND THE BEND.

COMING OUT OF THE CONVENTION, OBAMA SCORED A 6-POINT JUMP IN THE POLLS.

BUT THE REPUBLICAN NOMINEE, SENATOR JOHN McCAIN OF ARIZONA, CLAIMED THE MEDIA SPOTLIGHT THE MORNING AFTER OBAMA'S BIG SPEECH BY ANNOUNCING HIS VICE PRESIDENTIAL PICK, THE LITTLE KNOWN BUT CHARISMATIC GOVERNOR OF ALASKA, SARAH PALIN.

PALIN WAS LOOKED UPON AS A CONSERVATIVE WHO COULD HELP ENERGIZE THE RIGHT WING BASE THAT HAD SO FAR LACKED ENTHUSIASM FOR McCAIN'S CANDIDACY.

SHE'S EXACTLY WHO THIS COUNTRY NEEDS TO HELP ME FIGHT THE SAME OLD WASHINGTON POLITICS OF "ME FIRST AND COUNTRY SECOND."

THE REPUBLICAN NATIONAL CONVENTION WAS SCHEDULED TO START ON SEPTEMBER 1, THE SAME DAY HURRICANE GUSTAV BEGAN POUNDING LOUISIANA.

OBAMA ENCOURAGED GULF COAST RESIDENTS TO EVACUATE AND SOLICITED AID MONEY AND VOLUNTEERS.

McCAIN MADE A TRIP TO THE AREA SUNDAY, THE DAY BEFORE THE REPUBLICAN CONVENTION. HE CONSIDERED GIVING HIS ACCEPTANCE SPEECH FROM NEW ORLEANS BUT DECIDED AGAINST IT.

THE CONVENTION OPENED ON SCHEDULE BUT THE MOOD WAS SUBDUED. MONDAY'S EVENTS WERE CUT BY FOUR HOURS, NOT IN PRIME TIME, AND LARGELY DEVOTED TO RAISING MONEY AND AWARENESS FOR GUSTAV'S VICTIMS.

GUSTAV WAS AN UNFORTUNATE REMINDER OF ONE OF THE BUSH ADMINISTRATION'S WORST MOMENTS—THE SLOW AND MUDDLED RESPONSE TO HURRICANE KATRINA, THREE YEARS BEFORE.

WITH HIS JOB APPROVAL RATINGS HOVERING IN THE LOW 30s, BUSH WAS NOT A FIGURE McCAIN WANTED TO BE TIED TO.

LAURA BUSH AND CINDY McCAIN SPOKE, BUT A SCHEDULED SPEECH BY PRESIDENT GEORGE W. BUSH WAS CANCELLED. HE WOULD LATER ADDRESS THE CONVENTION BY VIDEO, BUT HE DID NOT ATTEND IN PERSON.

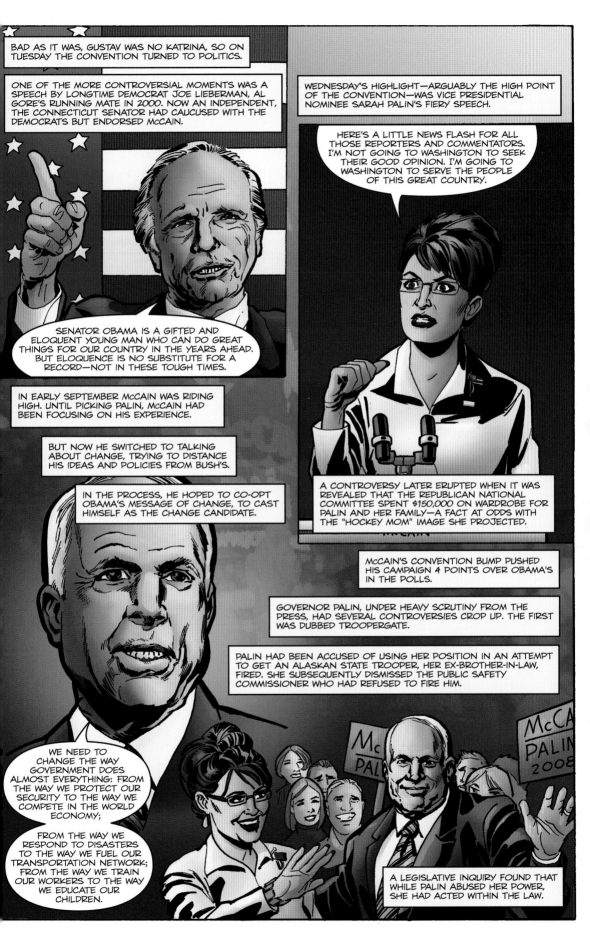

BAD AS IT WAS, GUSTAV WAS NO KATRINA, SO ON TUESDAY THE CONVENTION TURNED TO POLITICS.

ONE OF THE MORE CONTROVERSIAL MOMENTS WAS A SPEECH BY LONGTIME DEMOCRAT JOE LIEBERMAN, AL GORE'S RUNNING MATE IN 2000. NOW AN INDEPENDENT, THE CONNECTICUT SENATOR HAD CAUCUSED WITH THE DEMOCRATS BUT ENDORSED McCAIN.

WEDNESDAY'S HIGHLIGHT—ARGUABLY THE HIGH POINT OF THE CONVENTION—WAS VICE PRESIDENTIAL NOMINEE SARAH PALIN'S FIERY SPEECH.

HERE'S A LITTLE NEWS FLASH FOR ALL THOSE REPORTERS AND COMMENTATORS. I'M NOT GOING TO WASHINGTON TO SEEK THEIR GOOD OPINION. I'M GOING TO WASHINGTON TO SERVE THE PEOPLE OF THIS GREAT COUNTRY.

SENATOR OBAMA IS A GIFTED AND ELOQUENT YOUNG MAN WHO CAN DO GREAT THINGS FOR OUR COUNTRY IN THE YEARS AHEAD. BUT ELOQUENCE IS NO SUBSTITUTE FOR A RECORD—NOT IN THESE TOUGH TIMES.

IN EARLY SEPTEMBER McCAIN WAS RIDING HIGH. UNTIL PICKING PALIN, McCAIN HAD BEEN FOCUSING ON HIS EXPERIENCE.

BUT NOW HE SWITCHED TO TALKING ABOUT CHANGE, TRYING TO DISTANCE HIS IDEAS AND POLICIES FROM BUSH'S.

IN THE PROCESS, HE HOPED TO CO-OPT OBAMA'S MESSAGE OF CHANGE, TO CAST HIMSELF AS THE CHANGE CANDIDATE.

A CONTROVERSY LATER ERUPTED WHEN IT WAS REVEALED THAT THE REPUBLICAN NATIONAL COMMITTEE SPENT $150,000 ON WARDROBE FOR PALIN AND HER FAMILY—A FACT AT ODDS WITH THE "HOCKEY MOM" IMAGE SHE PROJECTED.

McCAIN'S CONVENTION BUMP PUSHED HIS CAMPAIGN 4 POINTS OVER OBAMA'S IN THE POLLS.

GOVERNOR PALIN, UNDER HEAVY SCRUTINY FROM THE PRESS, HAD SEVERAL CONTROVERSIES CROP UP. THE FIRST WAS DUBBED TROOPERGATE.

PALIN HAD BEEN ACCUSED OF USING HER POSITION IN AN ATTEMPT TO GET AN ALASKAN STATE TROOPER, HER EX-BROTHER-IN-LAW, FIRED. SHE SUBSEQUENTLY DISMISSED THE PUBLIC SAFETY COMMISSIONER WHO HAD REFUSED TO FIRE HIM.

WE NEED TO CHANGE THE WAY GOVERNMENT DOES ALMOST EVERYTHING: FROM THE WAY WE PROTECT OUR SECURITY TO THE WAY WE COMPETE IN THE WORLD ECONOMY;

FROM THE WAY WE RESPOND TO DISASTERS TO THE WAY WE FUEL OUR TRANSPORTATION NETWORK; FROM THE WAY WE TRAIN OUR WORKERS TO THE WAY WE EDUCATE OUR CHILDREN.

A LEGISLATIVE INQUIRY FOUND THAT WHILE PALIN ABUSED HER POWER, SHE HAD ACTED WITHIN THE LAW.

AND THERE WERE OTHER LANDMINES LYING IN WAIT, FOR BOTH CAMPAIGNS AND FOR THE AMERICAN ECONOMY.

AMERICA'S MORTGAGES WERE GOING INTO MELTDOWN. ON SEPTEMBER 7, THE BUSH ADMINISTRATION ANNOUNCED THAT MORTGAGE GIANTS FANNIE MAE AND FREDDIE MAC WOULD BE PLACED UNDER FEDERAL CONTROL, IN HOPES OF HEADING OFF A FULL-FLEDGED DISASTER.

FORECLOSURE
HOME FOR

THE ECONOMY WAS TEETERING, IN WAYS THAT WOULD PLAY OUT OVER THE DAYS AND WEEKS TO COME.

OBAMA RESPONDED WITH ADS POINTING OUT THAT FOR "MAVERICKS," THERE WERE AN AWFUL LOT OF LOBBYISTS WORKING ON THE McCAIN/PALIN CAMPAIGN. HE SAID McCAIN AND PALIN WERE "LYING ABOUT THEIR RECORDS," SPECIFICALLY ABOUT PALIN'S CONTINUED CLAIMS TO HAVE OPPOSED ALASKA'S FAMED "BRIDGE TO NOWHERE."

THERE WERE OCCASIONAL LIGHTER MOMENTS, INCLUDING FAKE PHOTOS ON THE INTERNET PURPORTEDLY SHOWING ONE-TIME BEAUTY QUEEN PALIN IN A STARS AND STRIPES BIKINI, BRANDISHING AN ASSAULT RIFLE.

AND TINA FEY'S HUGELY POPULAR STAR TURN AS PALIN ON *SATURDAY NIGHT LIVE* EVENTUALLY CULMINATED IN GUEST APPEARANCES ON THE LIVE SKETCH PROGRAM BY McCAIN AND PALIN. OBAMA ALSO MADE A CAMEO APPEARANCE ON THE SHOW.

BUT THESE WERE THE EXCEPTIONS—THE CAMPAIGNS WERE GROWING MORE AND MORE HEATED.

McCAIN HAD COME OUT OF THE CONVENTION ON THE OFFENSIVE, ACCUSING OBAMA OF PUTTING PERSONAL AMBITION AHEAD OF COUNTRY, OF SUPPORTING THE STATUS QUO WHILE HE AND PALIN WERE THE REAL REFORMERS.

SOME FELT THAT OBAMA'S REACTIONS WERE TOO SLOW, TOO TIMID. BY BEING ON THE DEFENSIVE RATHER THAN THE OFFENSIVE, HE WAS CEDING CONTROL OF THE RACE'S NARRATIVE TO McCAIN.

BUT OBAMA MAINTAINED THAT HE HAD A PLAN AND WAS STICKING TO IT.

THE MAINSTREAM MEDIA, WHO McCAIN HAD ONCE CALLED "MY [B]ASE," STARTED TO PICK UP OBAMA'S VERSION OF EVENTS.

AND WHILE SHE CLAIMED TO OPPOSE PORK BARREL SPENDING, SHE HAD A RECORD OF REQUESTING AND ACCEPTING EARMARK MONEY.

LEARNING ABOUT **SEX** BEFORE LEARNING TO **READ**

NOWHERE ALASKA 99901

[T]HEY REVEALED THAT PALIN'S OPPOSITION TO THE [B]RIDGE TO NOWHERE" DIDN'T COME ABOUT UNTIL [A]FTER CONGRESS HAD CUT FUNDING FOR IT. AS LONG [A]S IT WOULD BE PAID FOR BY FEDERAL MONEY [I]NSTEAD OF ALASKA MONEY, SHE HAD SUPPORTED IT.

THE McCAIN CAMPAIGN FOLLOWED WITH EVEN HARDER-HITTING ADS, INCLUDING A CONTROVERSIAL ONE ACCUSING OBAMA OF SUPPORTING SEX EDUCATION FOR KINDERGARTENERS.

AND WHEN OBAMA DESCRIBED McCAIN'S POLICIES AS "A PIG IN LIPSTICK"—A PHRASE McCAIN HAD USED WHEN REFERRING TO HILLARY CLINTON'S HEALTH CARE PLAN—McCAIN'S CAMPAIGN FIRED BACK, ASSERTING THAT OBAMA WAS BEING DISRESPECTFUL TOWARDS PALIN.

ON SEPTEMBER 11, THE ANNIVERSARY OF THE 2001 TERROR ATTACKS ON THE WORLD TRADE CENTER AND PENTAGON, THE TWO MEN PUT ASIDE THEIR DIFFERENCES AND APPEARED TOGETHER IN NEW YORK AT A CEREMONY COMMEMORATING THE TRAGEDY, AT GROUND ZERO.

AND THAT DAY CHARLIE GIBSON OF ABC NEWS CONDUCTED PALIN'S FIRST INTERVIEW SINCE BEING SELECTED.

WHAT INSIGHT INTO RUSSIAN ACTIONS, PARTICULARLY IN THE LAST COUPLE OF WEEKS, DOES THE PROXIMITY OF THE STATE GIVE YOU?

THEY'RE OUR NEXT-DOOR NEIGHBORS AND YOU CAN ACTUALLY SEE RUSSIA FROM LAND HERE IN ALASKA, FROM AN ISLAND IN ALASKA.

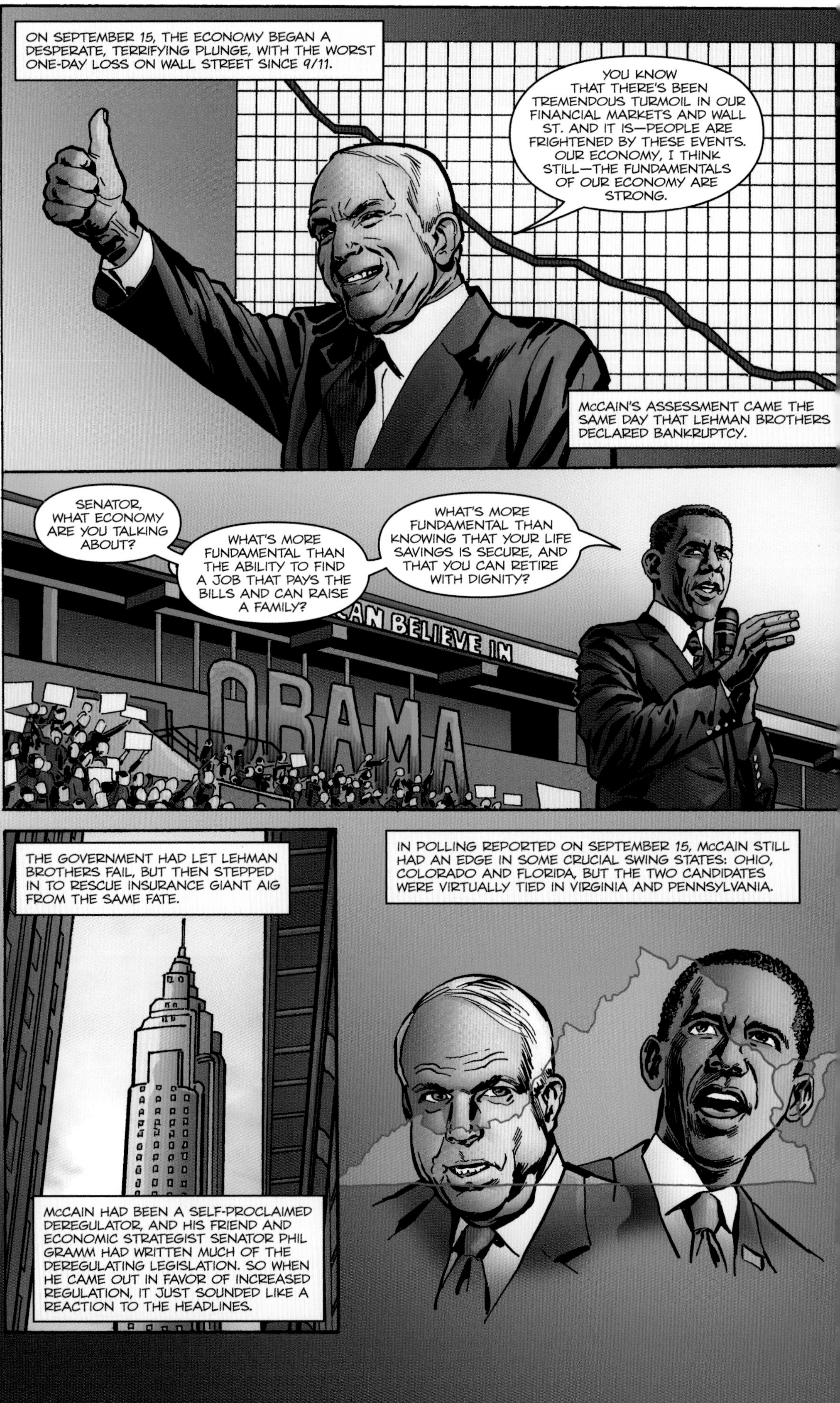

ON SEPTEMBER 15, THE ECONOMY BEGAN A DESPERATE, TERRIFYING PLUNGE, WITH THE WORST ONE-DAY LOSS ON WALL STREET SINCE 9/11.
YOU KNOW THAT THERE'S BEEN TREMENDOUS TURMOIL IN OUR FINANCIAL MARKETS AND WALL ST. AND IT IS—PEOPLE ARE FRIGHTENED BY THESE EVENTS. OUR ECONOMY, I THINK STILL—THE FUNDAMENTALS OF OUR ECONOMY ARE STRONG.
McCAIN'S ASSESSMENT CAME THE SAME DAY THAT LEHMAN BROTHERS DECLARED BANKRUPTCY.
SENATOR, WHAT ECONOMY ARE YOU TALKING ABOUT?
WHAT'S MORE FUNDAMENTAL THAN THE ABILITY TO FIND A JOB THAT PAYS THE BILLS AND CAN RAISE A FAMILY?
WHAT'S MORE FUNDAMENTAL THAN KNOWING THAT YOUR LIFE SAVINGS IS SECURE, AND THAT YOU CAN RETIRE WITH DIGNITY?
OBAMA
THE GOVERNMENT HAD LET LEHMAN BROTHERS FAIL, BUT THEN STEPPED IN TO RESCUE INSURANCE GIANT AIG FROM THE SAME FATE.
McCAIN HAD BEEN A SELF-PROCLAIMED DEREGULATOR, AND HIS FRIEND AND ECONOMIC STRATEGIST SENATOR PHIL GRAMM HAD WRITTEN MUCH OF THE DEREGULATING LEGISLATION. SO WHEN HE CAME OUT IN FAVOR OF INCREASED REGULATION, IT JUST SOUNDED LIKE A REACTION TO THE HEADLINES.
IN POLLING REPORTED ON SEPTEMBER 15, McCAIN STILL HAD AN EDGE IN SOME CRUCIAL SWING STATES: OHIO, COLORADO AND FLORIDA, BUT THE TWO CANDIDATES WERE VIRTUALLY TIED IN VIRGINIA AND PENNSYLVANIA.

BUT IN NATIONAL POLLING OBAMA WAS SURGING AHEAD.

THE ECONOMY HAD BECOME THE NUMBER ONE CONCERN IN THE RACE, THE MAJOR ISSUE AMERICANS HAD BECOME FOCUSED ON.

I CERTAINLY DON'T FAULT SENATOR McCAIN FOR ALL OF THE PROBLEMS WE'RE FACING, BUT I DO FAULT THE ECONOMIC PHILOSOPHY HE SUBSCRIBES TO.

CHANGE WE CAN BELIEVE I

THE BUSH ADMINISTRATION WANTED TO BAILOUT THE FINANCIAL SECTOR BEFORE IT COLLAPSED ENTIRELY. A BAIL OUT OF $700 BILLION WASN'T UNIVERSALLY POPULAR, BUT TREASURY SECRETARY HENRY PAULSON INSISTED IT WAS NECESSARY.

OBAMA SAID, "MAKE NO MISTAKE: MY OPPONENT IS RUNNING FOR FOUR MORE YEARS OF POLICIES THAT WILL THROW THE ECONOMY FURTHER OUT OF BALANCE. HIS OUTRAGE AT WALL STREET WOULD BE MORE CONVINCING IF HE WASN'T OFFERING THEM MORE TAX CUTS."

WILL WORK FOR ???

IN SPEECHES AND ADS, OBAMA ATTACKED McCAIN'S ECONOMIC RECORD AND QUESTIONED HIS SUDDEN CONVERSION TO POPULISM.

AND THE PUBLIC RESPONDED. A NATIONAL POLL SHOWED PEOPLE TRUSTED OBAMA MORE THAN McCAIN ON THE ECONOMY. OBAMA SURGED PAST 50% IN THAT POLL.

DUE TO THE FINANCIAL CRISIS, McCAIN ANNOUNCED THAT HE WOULD SUSPEND HIS CAMPAIGN AND RETURN TO WASHINGTON. OBAMA WENT TO WASHINGTON TOO, WHERE THE TWO MET WITH PRESIDENT BUSH AND PARTY LEADERS.

McCAIN THREATENED TO SKIP THE FIRST DEBATE, SCHEDULED FOR SEPTEMBER 26, IN CASE HE WAS NEEDED IN WASHINGTON. BUT THE COMMISSION ON PRESIDENTIAL DEBATES, THE EVENT'S SPONSORS, CONTINUED THEIR PREPARATIONS.

THE "SUSPENSION" TURNED OUT TO BE LARGELY IN NAME ONLY, AS McCAIN'S CAMPAIGN OFFICES REMAINED OPEN, TV ADS KEPT AIRING, AND SURROGATES CONTINUED TO APPEAR ON TV.

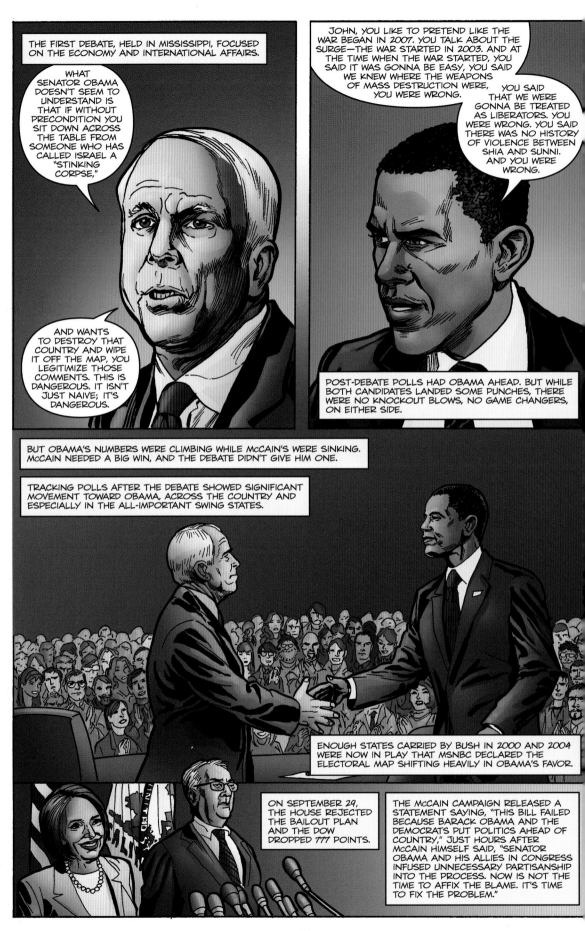

THE FIRST DEBATE, HELD IN MISSISSIPPI, FOCUSED ON THE ECONOMY AND INTERNATIONAL AFFAIRS.

WHAT SENATOR OBAMA DOESN'T SEEM TO UNDERSTAND IS THAT IF WITHOUT PRECONDITION YOU SIT DOWN ACROSS THE TABLE FROM SOMEONE WHO HAS CALLED ISRAEL A "STINKING CORPSE,"

AND WANTS TO DESTROY THAT COUNTRY AND WIPE IT OFF THE MAP, YOU LEGITIMIZE THOSE COMMENTS. THIS IS DANGEROUS. IT ISN'T JUST NAIVE; IT'S DANGEROUS.

JOHN, YOU LIKE TO PRETEND LIKE THE WAR BEGAN IN 2007. YOU TALK ABOUT THE SURGE—THE WAR STARTED IN 2003. AND AT THE TIME WHEN THE WAR STARTED, YOU SAID IT WAS GONNA BE EASY, YOU SAID WE KNEW WHERE THE WEAPONS OF MASS DESTRUCTION WERE, YOU WERE WRONG.

YOU SAID THAT WE WERE GONNA BE TREATED AS LIBERATORS. YOU WERE WRONG. YOU SAID THERE WAS NO HISTORY OF VIOLENCE BETWEEN SHIA AND SUNNI. AND YOU WERE WRONG.

POST-DEBATE POLLS HAD OBAMA AHEAD. BUT WHILE BOTH CANDIDATES LANDED SOME PUNCHES, THERE WERE NO KNOCKOUT BLOWS, NO GAME CHANGERS, ON EITHER SIDE.

BUT OBAMA'S NUMBERS WERE CLIMBING WHILE McCAIN'S WERE SINKING. McCAIN NEEDED A BIG WIN, AND THE DEBATE DIDN'T GIVE HIM ONE.

TRACKING POLLS AFTER THE DEBATE SHOWED SIGNIFICANT MOVEMENT TOWARD OBAMA, ACROSS THE COUNTRY AND ESPECIALLY IN THE ALL-IMPORTANT SWING STATES.

ENOUGH STATES CARRIED BY BUSH IN 2000 AND 2004 WERE NOW IN PLAY THAT MSNBC DECLARED THE ELECTORAL MAP SHIFTING HEAVILY IN OBAMA'S FAVOR.

ON SEPTEMBER 29, THE HOUSE REJECTED THE BAILOUT PLAN AND THE DOW DROPPED 777 POINTS.

THE McCAIN CAMPAIGN RELEASED A STATEMENT SAYING, "THIS BILL FAILED BECAUSE BARACK OBAMA AND THE DEMOCRATS PUT POLITICS AHEAD OF COUNTRY," JUST HOURS AFTER McCAIN HIMSELF SAID, "SENATOR OBAMA AND HIS ALLIES IN CONGRESS INFUSED UNNECESSARY PARTISANSHIP INTO THE PROCESS. NOW IS NOT THE TIME TO AFFIX THE BLAME. IT'S TIME TO FIX THE PROBLEM."

IN OCTOBER THE VP CANDIDATES TOOK CENTER STAGE. THEIR ONLY DEBATE WOULD BE HELD OCTOBER 2 IN ST. LOUIS. GOVERNOR PALIN'S INTERVIEW WITH KATIE COURIC HAD BEEN AIRING THROUGHOUT THE WEEK.

WHEN IT COMES TO ESTABLISHING YOUR WORLDVIEW, I WAS CURIOUS, WHAT NEWSPAPERS AND MAGAZINES DID YOU REGULARLY READ BEFORE YOU WERE TAPPED FOR THIS, TO STAY INFORMED AND TO UNDERSTAND THE WORLD?

I'VE READ MOST OF THEM, AGAIN WITH A GREAT APPRECIATION FOR THE PRESS, FOR THE MEDIA.

WHAT, SPECIFICALLY?

UM, ALL OF THEM, ANY OF THEM THAT HAVE BEEN IN FRONT OF ME ALL THESE YEARS.

MORE VIEWERS TUNED IN FOR THE VP DEBATE THAN HAD FOR THE PRESIDENTIAL ONE.

OBAMA WATCHED SENATOR BIDEN AND GOVERNOR PALIN SQUARE OFF FROM A HOTEL ROOM IN MICHIGAN WHILE McCAIN WATCHED FROM HIS HOTEL IN THE SWING STATE OF COLORADO.

BOTH CANDIDATES GOT SOME GOOD SHOTS IN, BUT NOTHING DECISIVE. BIDEN STRESSED HIS EXPERIENCE AND KNOWLEDGE, WHILE PALIN PLAYED UP HER FOLKSINESS AND MAVERICK REPUTATION.

ASK ANYBODY... WHETHER OR NOT THE ECONOMIC AND FOREIGN POLICY OF THIS ADMINISTRATION HAS MADE THEM BETTER OFF IN THE LAST EIGHT YEARS.

ON TAXES, ON IRAQ, ON AFGHANISTAN, ON THE WHOLE QUESTION OF HOW TO HELP EDUCATION, ON THE DEALING WITH HEALTH CARE.

AND THEN ASK THEM WHETHER THERE'S A SINGLE MAJOR INITIATIVE THAT JOHN McCAIN DIFFERS WITH THE PRESIDENT ON.

SAY IT AIN'T SO, JOE. THERE YOU GO AGAIN POINTING BACKWARDS AGAIN. YOU PREFERENCED YOUR WHOLE COMMENT WITH THE BUSH ADMINISTRATION.

NOW DOGGONE IT, LET'S LOOK AHEAD AND TELL AMERICANS WHAT WE HAVE TO PLAN TO DO FOR THEM IN THE FUTURE.

PUNDITS WERE IMPRESSED WITH PALIN'S PERFORMANCE, BUT VIEWERS PICKED BIDEN AS THE WINNER, ACCORDING TO THE POST-DEBATE POLLS.

WHEN THE DEBATES FAILED TO CHANGE THE TRAJECTORY, THE McCAIN CAMP ANNOUNCED THAT IT WANTED TO STOP TALKING ABOUT THE ECONOMY AND FOCUS ON OBAMA'S CHARACTER.

PALIN FIRED THE FIRST SHOT, BRINGING UP FORMER RADICAL WILLIAM AYERS.

THIS IS NOT A MAN WHO SEES AMERICA AS YOU AND I DO—AS THE GREATEST FORCE FOR GOOD IN THE WORLD.

THIS IS SOMEONE WHO SEES AMERICA AS IMPERFECT ENOUGH TO PAL AROUND WITH TERRORISTS WHO TARGETED THEIR OWN COUNTRY.

McCA

PALIN

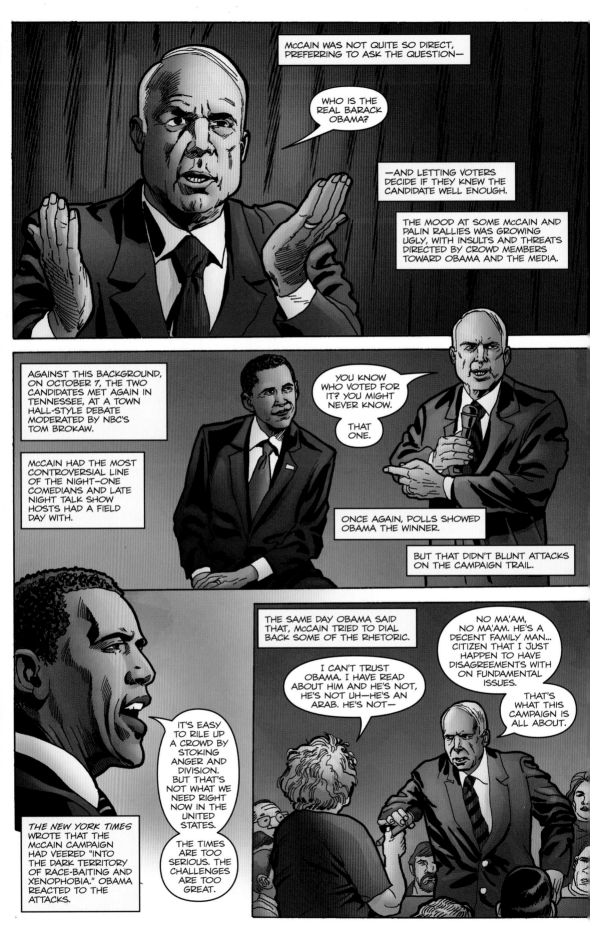

MCCAIN WAS NOT QUITE SO DIRECT, PREFERRING TO ASK THE QUESTION—

WHO IS THE REAL BARACK OBAMA?

—AND LETTING VOTERS DECIDE IF THEY KNEW THE CANDIDATE WELL ENOUGH.

THE MOOD AT SOME McCAIN AND PALIN RALLIES WAS GROWING UGLY, WITH INSULTS AND THREATS DIRECTED BY CROWD MEMBERS TOWARD OBAMA AND THE MEDIA.

AGAINST THIS BACKGROUND, ON OCTOBER 7, THE TWO CANDIDATES MET AGAIN IN TENNESSEE, AT A TOWN HALL-STYLE DEBATE MODERATED BY NBC'S TOM BROKAW.

McCAIN HAD THE MOST CONTROVERSIAL LINE OF THE NIGHT—ONE COMEDIANS AND LATE NIGHT TALK SHOW HOSTS HAD A FIELD DAY WITH.

YOU KNOW WHO VOTED FOR IT? YOU MIGHT NEVER KNOW.

THAT ONE.

ONCE AGAIN, POLLS SHOWED OBAMA THE WINNER.

BUT THAT DIDN'T BLUNT ATTACKS ON THE CAMPAIGN TRAIL.

THE SAME DAY OBAMA SAID THAT, McCAIN TRIED TO DIAL BACK SOME OF THE RHETORIC.

I CAN'T TRUST OBAMA. I HAVE READ ABOUT HIM AND HE'S NOT, HE'S NOT UH—HE'S AN ARAB. HE'S NOT—

NO MA'AM, NO MA'AM. HE'S A DECENT FAMILY MAN... CITIZEN THAT I JUST HAPPEN TO HAVE DISAGREEMENTS WITH ON FUNDAMENTAL ISSUES.

THAT'S WHAT THIS CAMPAIGN IS ALL ABOUT.

IT'S EASY TO RILE UP A CROWD BY STOKING ANGER AND DIVISION. BUT THAT'S NOT WHAT WE NEED RIGHT NOW IN THE UNITED STATES.

THE TIMES ARE TOO SERIOUS. THE CHALLENGES ARE TOO GREAT.

THE NEW YORK TIMES WROTE THAT THE McCAIN CAMPAIGN HAD VEERED "INTO THE DARK TERRITORY OF RACE-BAITING AND XENOPHOBIA." OBAMA REACTED TO THE ATTACKS.

BEHIND IN ALL THE POLLS, McCAIN SOUNDED AN OPTIMISTIC NOTE.

LET ME GIVE YOU THE STATE OF THE RACE TODAY. WE HAVE 22 DAYS TO GO. WE'RE 6 POINTS DOWN. THE NATIONAL MEDIA HAS WRITTEN US OFF.

SENATOR OBAMA IS MEASURING THE DRAPES, AND PLANNING WITH SPEAKER PELOSI AND SENATOR REID TO RAISE TAXES, INCREASE SPENDING, TAKE AWAY YOUR RIGHT TO VOTE BY SECRET BALLOT IN LABOR ELECTIONS, AND CONCEDE DEFEAT IN IRAQ.

BUT THEY FORGOT TO LET YOU DECIDE. MY FRIENDS, WE'VE GOT THEM JUST WHERE WE WANT THEM...

OBAMA, MEANWHILE, SHARPENED HIS ECONOMIC MESSAGE WITH MORE SPECIFICS.

IT'S A PLAN THAT BEGINS WITH ONE WORD THAT'S ON EVERYONE'S MIND, AND IT'S SPELLED J-O-B-S.

WHILE TRYING TO STRIKE A HOPEFUL TONE, HE REMINDED AUDIENCES HOW HARD THE ROAD TO RECOVERY WOULD BE.

DURING THE DEBATE, McCAIN DESCRIBED THE LIBERAL GROUP ACORN AS "NOW ON THE VERGE OF MAYBE PERPETRATING ONE OF THE GREATEST FRAUDS IN VOTER HISTORY."

MULTIPLE INVESTIGATIONS REVEALED NO VOTER FRAUD. ACORN, WHO PAID WORKERS PER COMPLETED REGISTRATION FORM, THEMSELVES REPORTED THE FALSE REGISTRATIONS.

AS THE CANDIDATES PREPARED FOR THEIR THIRD AND FINAL DEBATE, THE TONE AT A PALIN RALLY TURNED UGLY.

BEFORE PALIN WENT ON, A CONGRESSIONAL CANDIDATE MENTIONED OBAMA'S NAME AND A MEMBER OF THE CROWD SHOUTED "KILL HIM!" PROMPTING A SECRET SERVICE INVESTIGATION.

THE LAST DEBATE TOOK PLACE IN NEW YORK. ALTHOUGH HE WASN'T THERE, IT WAS DOMINATED BY JOE THE PLUMBER, AN OHIO MAN WHO FEARED OBAMA WOULD RAISE HIS TAXES.

JOE THE PLUMBER WOULD BECOME A FIXTURE OF McCAIN RALLIES FOR THE REST OF THE CAMPAIGN.

AS IN THE PREVIOUS MEETINGS, OBAMA CAME ACROSS AS COOL, COLLECTED, AND PRESIDENTIAL.

THE FOLLOWING NIGHT THE MOOD WAS CONSIDERABLY LIGHTER AS THE CONTENDERS MET AT THE ANNUAL ALFRED E. SMITH DINNER.

THIS MORNING, I'VE DISMISSED MY ENTIRE TEAM OF SENIOR ADVISERS. ALL THEIR POSITIONS WILL NOW BE HELD BY A MAN NAMED JOE THE PLUMBER.

JOE THE PLUMBER RECENTLY SIGNED A VERY LUCRATIVE CONTRACT WITH A WEALTHY COUPLE TO HANDLE ALL THE WORK ON ALL SEVEN OF THEIR HOUSES.

LIFELONG COMIC BOOK FAN OBAMA GOT IN SOME GOOD LINES OF HIS OWN.

CONTRARY TO THE RUMORS YOU HAVE HEARD, I WAS NOT BORN IN A MANGER. I WAS ACTUALLY BORN ON KRYPTON AND SENT HERE BY MY FATHER, JOR-EL, TO SAVE THE PLANET EARTH.

I FEEL RIGHT AT HOME HERE BECAUSE IT'S OFTEN BEEN SAID THAT I SHARE THE POLITICS OF ALFRED E. SMITH AND THE EARS OF ALFRED E. NEUMAN.

QUESTIONABLE CAMPAIGN TACTICS AND PERCEIVED STUNTS TURNED SEVERAL HIGH PROFILE CONSERVATIVES AGAINST McCAIN.

ON OCTOBER 19, GENERAL COLIN POWELL, FORMER SECRETARY OF STATE IN THE BUSH ADMINISTRATION, ENDORSED OBAMA.

I THINK WE NEED A GENERATIONAL CHANGE. AND I THINK SENATOR OBAMA HAS CAPTURED THE FEELINGS OF THE YOUNG PEOPLE OF AMERICA AND IS REACHING OUT IN A MORE DIVERSE, INCLUSIVE WAY ACROSS OUR SOCIETY.

MEANWHILE, PALIN GAVE VOICE TO ANOTHER LINE OF ATTACK THAT WOULD CONTINUE THROUGH THE REST OF THE CAMPAIGN.

BARACK OBAMA CALLS IT SPREADING THE WEALTH. JOE BIDEN CALLS HIGHER TAXES PATRIOTIC.

BUT JOE THE PLUMBER AND ED THE DAIRYMAN, I BELIEVE THAT THEY THINK THAT IT SOUNDS MORE LIKE SOCIALISM.

FRIENDS, NOW IS NO TIME TO EXPERIMENT WITH SOCIALISM.

TWO WEEKS BEFORE ELECTION DAY, VOTING BEGAN IN EARNEST, WITH EARLY OR ABSENTEE VOTES CAST IN EVERY STATE. EXIT POLLS AND ABSENTEE BALLOT REQUESTS IN BATTLEGROUND STATES RAN HEAVILY IN OBAMA'S FAVOR.

ON OCTOBER 23-24, OBAMA CANCELED HIS APPEARANCES AND FLEW TO HAWAII. HIS GRANDMOTHER, MADELYN DUNHAM—WHO HE CALLED TOOT, AND WHO HAD LARGELY RAISED HIM DURING HIS MOTHER'S LONG ABSENCES—HAD CANCER, AND HER HEALTH HAD TAKEN A DRAMATIC TURN FOR THE WORSE.

LATER, OBAMA WOULD TELL *TIME* MAGAZINE, "SHE REALLY GREW UP IN THE DEPRESSION, IN A SMALL TOWN IN KANSAS, AND NEVER GOT A COLLEGE DEGREE.

"SOMEHOW FOUND HERSELF IN HAWAII. SOMEHOW FOUND HER DAUGHTER MARRYING AN AFRICAN GUY. RAISED THIS MIXED KID WHO GOT IN ALL KINDS OF TROUBLE DURING HIS TEENAGE YEARS.

"YOU KNOW, THE LIKELIHOOD OF THAT LITTLE BOY ENDING UP PRESIDENT OF THE UNITED STATES WAS PRETTY LOW."

SPEAKING IN SEATTLE, BIDEN SEEMED TO HAND McCAIN SOME AMMUNITION.

MARK MY WORDS. IT WILL NOT BE SIX MONTHS BEFORE THE WORLD TESTS BARACK OBAMA LIKE THEY DID JOHN KENNEDY.

THE WORLD IS LOOKING. WE'RE ABOUT TO ELECT A BRILLIANT 47-YEAR-OLD SENATOR PRESIDENT OF THE UNITED STATES OF AMERICA.

McCAIN JUMPED ON THE STATEMENT, BUT A BIDEN SPOKESPERSON AND OBAMA BOTH ASSERTED THAT BIDEN MEANT THAT ANY PRESIDENT WOULD BE TESTED, AND OBAMA WOULD RISE TO ANY CHALLENGE.

PERHAPS THE MOST SHOCKING STORY OF THE CAMPAIGN BROKE IN PENNSYLVANIA, A CRUCIAL STATE FOR McCAIN, WHEN A 20-YEAR-OLD WHITE McCAIN VOLUNTEER TOLD POLICE THAT A BLACK MAN ASSAULTED HER AND CUT A BACKWARDS "B" ON HER CHEEK.

THE WOMAN SOON CONFESSED TO MAKING THE STORY UP AND CUTTING HERSELF. POLICE WERE SUSPICIOUS BECAUSE THE B WAS BACKWARDS, AS IF DONE WHILE LOOKING IN A MIRROR.

HAVING BEEN AHEAD IN THE POLLS FOR WEEKS, BY OCTOBER 27 OBAMA WAS READY TO SEAL THE DEAL. HE GAVE A MAJOR SPEECH BILLED AS HIS "CLOSING ARGUMENT."

IN ONE WEEK, WE CAN CHOOSE AN ECONOMY THAT REWARDS WORK AND CREATES NEW JOBS AND FUELS PROSPERITY FROM THE BOTTOM UP.

IN ONE WEEK, WE CAN CHOOSE TO INVEST IN HEALTH CARE FOR OUR FAMILIES, AND EDUCATION FOR OUR KIDS, AND RENEWABLE ENERGY FOR OUR FUTURE.

IN ONE WEEK, WE CAN CHOOSE HOPE OVER FEAR, UNITY OVER DIVISION, THE PROMISE OF CHANGE OVER THE POWER OF THE STATUS QUO.

IN ONE WEEK, WE CAN COME TOGETHER AS ONE NATION, AND ONE PEOPLE, AND ONCE MORE CHOOSE OUR BETTER HISTORY.

JOHN McCAIN HAD STARTED REFERRING TO OBAMA AS "BARACK THE REDISTRIBUTOR."

OBAMA STRUCK BACK WITH HUMOR.

BY THE END OF THE WEEK, HE'LL BE ACCUSING ME OF BEING A SECRET COMMUNIST BECAUSE I SHARED MY TOYS IN KINDERGARTEN.

I SHARED MY PEANUT BUTTER AND JELLY SANDWICH.

ON OCTOBER 29, OBAMA BOUGHT 30 MINUTES OF AIR-TIME ON SEVEN TELEVISION NETWORKS AND CABLE CHANNELS. ALMOST 34 MILLION PEOPLE WATCHED.

THE "INFOMERCIAL" WAS DESIGNED TO MAKE HIM LOOK PRESIDENTIAL, TO ELIMINATE ANY REMAINING DOUBTS ABOUT HIS READINESS FOR THE JOB.

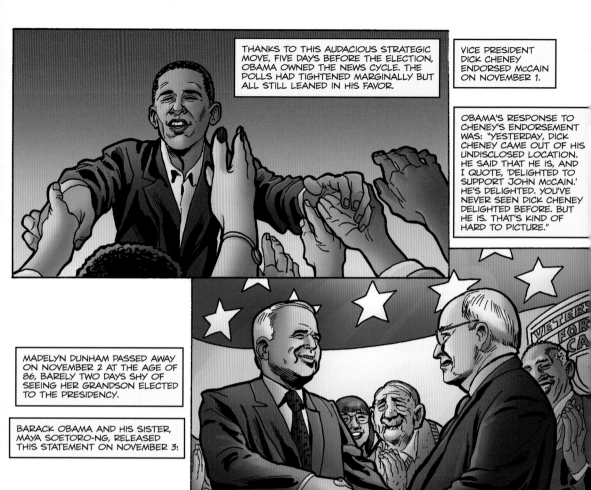

THANKS TO THIS AUDACIOUS STRATEGIC MOVE, FIVE DAYS BEFORE THE ELECTION, OBAMA OWNED THE NEWS CYCLE. THE POLLS HAD TIGHTENED MARGINALLY BUT ALL STILL LEANED IN HIS FAVOR.

VICE PRESIDENT DICK CHENEY ENDORSED McCAIN ON NOVEMBER 1.

OBAMA'S RESPONSE TO CHENEY'S ENDORSEMENT WAS: "YESTERDAY, DICK CHENEY CAME OUT OF HIS UNDISCLOSED LOCATION. HE SAID THAT HE IS, AND I QUOTE, 'DELIGHTED TO SUPPORT JOHN McCAIN.' HE'S DELIGHTED. YOU'VE NEVER SEEN DICK CHENEY DELIGHTED BEFORE. BUT HE IS. THAT'S KIND OF HARD TO PICTURE."

MADELYN DUNHAM PASSED AWAY ON NOVEMBER 2 AT THE AGE OF 86, BARELY TWO DAYS SHY OF SEEING HER GRANDSON ELECTED TO THE PRESIDENCY.

BARACK OBAMA AND HIS SISTER, MAYA SOETORO-NG, RELEASED THIS STATEMENT ON NOVEMBER 3:

"IT IS WITH GREAT SADNESS THAT WE ANNOUNCE THAT OUR GRANDMOTHER, MADELYN DUNHAM, HAS DIED PEACEFULLY AFTER A BATTLE WITH CANCER. SHE WAS THE CORNERSTONE OF OUR FAMILY, AND A WOMAN OF EXTRAORDINARY ACCOMPLISHMENT, STRENGTH, AND HUMILITY. SHE WAS THE PERSON WHO ENCOURAGED AND ALLOWED US TO TAKE CHANCES. SHE WAS PROUD OF HER GRANDCHILDREN AND GREAT-GRANDCHILDREN AND LEFT THIS WORLD WITH THE KNOWLEDGE THAT HER IMPACT ON ALL OF US WAS MEANINGFUL AND ENDURING. OUR DEBT TO HER IS BEYOND MEASURE.

"OUR FAMILY WANTS TO THANK ALL OF THOSE WHO SENT FLOWERS, CARDS, WELL-WISHES, AND PRAYERS DURING THIS DIFFICULT TIME. IT BROUGHT OUR GRANDMOTHER AND US GREAT COMFORT. OUR GRANDMOTHER WAS A PRIVATE WOMAN, AND WE WILL RESPECT HER WISH FOR A SMALL PRIVATE CEREMONY TO BE HELD AT A LATER DATE. IN LIEU OF FLOWERS, WE ASK THAT YOU MAKE A DONATION TO ANY WORTHY ORGANIZATION IN SEARCH OF A CURE FOR CANCER."

JOHN AND CINDY McCAIN RELEASED THIS STATEMENT: "WE OFFER OUR DEEPEST CONDOLENCES TO BARACK OBAMA AND HIS FAMILY AS THEY GRIEVE THE LOSS OF THEIR BELOVED GRANDMOTHER. OUR THOUGHTS AND PRAYERS GO OUT TO THEM AS THEY REMEMBER AND CELEBRATE THE LIFE OF SOMEONE WHO HAD SUCH A PROFOUND IMPACT IN THEIR LIVES."

ON NOVEMBER 4, AMERICANS WENT TO THE POLLS IN MASSIVE NUMBERS. THE CANDIDATES HAD SPENT THE LAST SEVERAL DAYS COVERING MANY STATES, EACH ONE INTENDING TO FINISH UP ELECTION DAY IN HIS HOME STATE—ILLINOIS FOR OBAMA, ARIZONA FOR McCAIN.

THE EXCITEMENT IN THE COUNTRY WAS PALPABLE. THIS HISTORIC CONTEST HAD BEEN LONG AND TENSE. WHATEVER THE OUTCOME, THE UNITED STATES WOULD NEVER BE THE SAME.

THE NIGHT'S FIRST MAJOR NEWS HAD PENNSYLVANIA BEING CALLED FOR OBAMA AT 8 PM ET. THE McCAIN CAMPAIGN HAD PUT A LOT OF WORK AND MONEY INTO THE KEYSTONE STATE, AND MANY ANALYSTS FELT THEIR PATH TO 270 ELECTORAL VOTES—THE NUMBER NEEDED TO SECURE A VICTORY—DEPENDED ON IT.

WHEN OBAMA TOOK OHIO, McCAIN'S CHANCES NARROWED EVEN MORE.

FINALLY, AT 11 PM ET, VIRGINIA FELL TO OBAMA, AND THE RACE WAS ESSENTIALLY OVER.

THE STATES KEPT FALLING INTO OBAMA'S COLUMN IN WHAT WOULD BECOME AN ELECTORAL LANDSLIDE.

McCAIN CALLED OBAMA TO CONCEDE AND THEN GAVE A GRACIOUS SPEECH TO SUPPORTERS.

I URGE ALL AMERICANS WHO SUPPORTED ME TO JOIN ME IN NOT JUST CONGRATULATING HIM, BUT OFFERING OUR NEXT PRESIDENT OUR GOODWILL AND EARNEST EFFORT TO FIND WAYS TO COME TOGETHER.

AND OBAMA ADDRESSED A CROWD ESTIMATED TO BE MORE THAN 100,000 IN CHICAGO'S GRANT PARK.

IF THERE IS ANYONE OUT THERE WHO STILL DOUBTS THAT AMERICA IS A PLACE WHERE ALL THINGS ARE POSSIBLE; WHO STILL WONDERS IF THE DREAM OF OUR FOUNDERS IS ALIVE IN OUR TIME; WHO STILL QUESTIONS THE POWER OF OUR DEMOCRACY, TONIGHT IS YOUR ANSWER.

IT'S THE ANSWER TOLD BY LINES THAT STRETCHED AROUND SCHOOLS AND CHURCHES IN NUMBERS THIS NATION HAS NEVER SEEN; BY PEOPLE WHO WAITED THREE HOURS AND FOUR HOURS, MANY FOR THE VERY FIRST TIME IN THEIR LIVES, BECAUSE THEY BELIEVED THAT THIS TIME MUST BE DIFFERENT; THAT THEIR VOICE COULD BE THAT DIFFERENCE.

IT'S THE ANSWER SPOKEN BY YOUNG AND OLD, RICH AND POOR, DEMOCRAT AND REPUBLICAN, BLACK, WHITE, LATINO, ASIAN, NATIVE AMERICAN, GAY, STRAIGHT, DISABLED AND NOT DISABLED - AMERICANS WHO SENT A MESSAGE TO THE WORLD THAT WE HAVE NEVER BEEN A COLLECTION OF RED STATES AND BLUE STATES: WE ARE, AND ALWAYS WILL BE, THE UNITED STATES OF AMERICA.

IT'S THE ANSWER THAT LED THOSE WHO HAVE BEEN TOLD FOR SO LONG BY SO MANY TO BE CYNICAL, AND FEARFUL, AND DOUBTFUL OF WHAT WE CAN ACHIEVE TO PUT THEIR HANDS ON THE ARC OF HISTORY AND BEND IT ONCE MORE TOWARD THE HOPE OF A BETTER DAY.

IT'S BEEN A LONG TIME COMING, BUT TONIGHT, BECAUSE OF WHAT WE DID ON THIS DAY, IN THIS ELECTION, AT THIS DEFINING MOMENT, CHANGE HAS COME TO AMERICA.

AND TO ALL THOSE WATCHING TONIGHT FROM BEYOND OUR SHORES, FROM PARLIAMENTS AND PALACES TO THOSE WHO ARE HUDDLED AROUND RADIOS IN THE FORGOTTEN CORNERS OF OUR WORLD—OUR STORIES ARE SINGULAR, BUT OUR DESTINY IS SHARED, AND A NEW DAWN OF AMERICAN LEADERSHIP IS AT HAND.
TO THOSE WHO WOULD TEAR THIS WORLD DOWN—WE WILL DEFEAT YOU.
TO THOSE WHO SEEK PEACE AND SECURITY—WE SUPPORT YOU.
AND TO ALL THOSE WHO HAVE WONDERED IF AMERICA'S BEACON STILL BURNS AS BRIGHT—TONIGHT WE PROVED ONCE MORE THAT THE TRUE STRENGTH OF OUR NATION COMES NOT FROM THE MIGHT OF OUR ARMS OR THE SCALE OF OUR WEALTH, BUT FROM THE ENDURING POWER OF OUR IDEALS: DEMOCRACY, LIBERTY, OPPORTUNITY, AND UNYIELDING HOPE.
THIS IS OUR MOMENT. THIS IS OUR TIME—TO PUT OUR PEOPLE BACK TO WORK AND OPEN DOORS OF OPPORTUNITY FOR OUR KIDS; TO RESTORE PROSPERITY AND PROMOTE THE CAUSE OF PEACE; TO RECLAIM THE AMERICAN DREAM AND REAFFIRM THAT FUNDAMENTAL TRUTH—
—THAT OUT OF MANY, WE ARE ONE; THAT WHILE WE BREATHE, WE HOPE, AND WHERE WE ARE MET WITH CYNICISM, AND DOUBT, AND THOSE WHO TELL US THAT WE CAN'T, WE WILL RESPOND WITH THAT TIMELESS CREED THAT SUMS UP THE SPIRIT OF A PEOPLE:
YES WE CAN. THANK YOU, GOD BLESS YOU, AND MAY GOD BLESS THE UNITED STATES OF AMERICA.
STATISTICS DO NOT CAPTURE THE JUBILATION THAT SWEPT ACROSS THE COUNTRY, AND AROUND THE WORLD, THAT NIGHT.
OBAMA WON 365 ELECTORAL VOTES TO McCAIN'S 173. HE WON MORE VOTES THAN ANY PRESIDENTIAL CANDIDATE IN HISTORY, FOR A POPULAR VOTE VICTORY OF 53% TO 46%. HE WON STATES IN EVERY REGION OF THE COUNTRY, SOME THAT DEMOCRATS HAD NOT WON IN DECADES.
THE FLOOD WASHED OTHER PARTY CANDIDATES INTO OFFICE, PUSHING THE DEMOCRATIC ADVANTAGE IN THE SENATE TO 58-41 (PENDING THE OUTCOME OF A STILL-DEBATED MINNESOTA CONTEST), AND IN THE HOUSE TO 257-178.
HISTORY HAD BEEN MADE.

THE MORNING OF JANUARY 20, 2009, DAWNED COLD AND CLEAR IN WASHINGTON, DC.

PEOPLE HAD BEEN FLOODING INTO THE CITY FOR DAYS, MORE THAN A MILLION OF EVERY AGE, RACE, AND COLOR PACKED THE NATIONAL MALL AND THE BLOCKS AROUND IT, ALL EAGER TO BE A PART OF THIS HISTORIC MOMENT.

THE PRESIDENT-ELECT CAME BY RAIL FROM PENNSYLVANIA, DUPLICATING, IN ABBREVIATED FORM, THE TRIP ABRAHAM LINCOLN MADE TO HIS INAUGURATION.

THE TRAIN STOPPED IN WILMINGTON, DELAWARE, TO PICK UP THE VICE PRESIDENT-ELECT. THRONGS GATHERED ALONG THE ROUTE, HOPING FOR A GLIMPSE OF THEIR NEXT PRESIDENT.

THROUGHOUT THE CAPITAL CITY PEOPLE GATHERED—FROM EVERY WALK OF LIFE, REGARDLESS OF ECONOMIC OR SOCIAL STATUS.

THE JOURNEY TO THIS POINT—EVEN THE JOURNEY FROM ELECTION DAY—HAD BEEN A LONG ONE.

THE OBAMA FAMILY KNEW THAT HIS ELECTION WOULD CHANGE THEIR LIVES DRASTICALLY. FOR ONE THING, OBAMA HAD BEEN A SENATOR AND A CANDIDATE FOR YEARS, RARELY HOME FOR DINNER.

FROM NOW ON THE FAMILY WOULD EAT DINNER TOGETHER, MORE OFTEN THAN NOT.

AND HIS DAUGHTERS MALIA AND SASHA HAD BEEN PROMISED A DOG, WIN OR LOSE.

BUT WITH THE ECONOMY IN FREE FALL AND TWO WARS UNDER WAY, OBAMA HAD TO GET STARTED ON THE SERIOUS BUSINESS AT HAND. HIS FIRST STEP: PICKING ILLINOIS REPRESENTATIVE RAHM EMANUEL AS HIS CHIEF OF STAFF.

DAYS LATER HE MET WITH PRESIDENT BUSH, WHO PLEDGED TO MAKE THE TRANSITION AS SMOOTH AS POSSIBLE.

IT WAS OBAMA'S FIRST VISIT TO THE OVAL OFFICE. LAURA BUSH SHOWED MICHELLE OBAMA THE FAMILY'S NEW RESIDENCE.

AND THERE WAS MUCH MORE TO DO, AS OBAMA TOLD A 60 MINUTES REPORTER.

NUMBER ONE, I THINK IT'S IMPORTANT TO GET A NATIONAL SECURITY TEAM IN PLACE BECAUSE TRANSITION PERIODS ARE POTENTIALLY TIMES OF VULNERABILITY TO A TERRORIST ATTACK.

WE WANNA MAKE SURE THAT THERE IS AS SEAMLESS A TRANSITION ON NATIONAL SECURITY AS POSSIBLE. OBVIOUSLY THE ECONOMY.

TALKING TO TOP ECONOMIC ADVISORS ABOUT HOW WE'RE GONNA CREATE JOBS, HOW WE GET THE ECONOMY BACK ON TRACK AND WHAT DO WE DO IN TERMS OF SOME LONG-TERM ISSUES LIKE ENERGY AND HEALTHCARE.

THE WEEKEND PRECEDING THE INAUGURATION WAS A TIME OF CELEBRATION AND COMMEMORATION (INCLUDING MICHELLE OBAMA'S 45TH BIRTHDAY, ON JANUARY 17).

SUNDAY BEGAN WITH CHURCH SERVICES, THEN A TRIP TO ARLINGTON NATIONAL CEMETERY.

A SPECTACULAR CONCERT AT THE LINCOLN MEMORIAL CAPPED THE DAY, WITH A STELLAR LINEUP OF PERFORMERS AND SPEAKERS THAT INCLUDED:

DENZEL WASHINGTON, MARTIN LUTHER KING III, JAMES TAYLOR, JOHN MELLENCAMP, MARY J. BLIGE, TIGER WOODS, GARTH BROOKS, STEVIE WONDER, U2, BRUCE SPRINGSTEEN AND PETE SEEGER, AMONG MANY OTHERS.

ISRAEL SUSPENDED MILITARY ACTION IN GAZA, PLANNING TO HAVE ALL THEIR TROOPS WITHDRAWN BY THE TIME OBAMA WAS SWORN IN.

THE SENATE HAD ALREADY RELEASED THE SECOND ROUND OF TARP* FUNDS, AIDING FINANCIAL INSTITUTIONS IN DISTRESS, AT OBAMA'S REQUEST. HE HAD NOT YET TAKEN OFFICE BUT HIS IMPACT WAS ALREADY BEING FELT.

*TROUBLED ASSET RELIEF PROGRAM

MONDAY WAS MARTIN LUTHER KING JR. DAY. OBAMA VISITED WOUNDED VETERANS AT WALTER REED HOSPITAL AND THEN WENT TO AN EMERGENCY SHELTER FOR HOMELESS TEENS AND PITCHED IN.

I THINK I'VE GOT THIS WALL COVERED.

LATER THAT NIGHT HE ATTENDED DINNERS IN HONOR OF VICE PRESIDENT-ELECT JOE BIDEN, FORMER OPPONENT SENATOR JOHN McCAIN, AND COLIN POWELL.

WITH MUCH TO ACCOMPLISH BETWEEN ELECTION AND INAUGURATION, OBAMA HAD WASTED NO TIME CHOOSING HIS CABINET. HIS NATIONAL SECURITY TEAM WOULD INCLUDE:

HILLARY CLINTON (SECRETARY OF STATE), ROBERT GATES (DEFENSE SECRETARY), GENERAL JAMES JONES (NATIONAL SECURITY ADVISOR), SUSAN RICE (U.N. AMBASSADOR), ERIC HOLDER JR. (ATTORNEY GENERAL), AND GOVERNOR JANET NAPOLITANO (HOMELAND SECURITY SECRETARY).

THE GOVERNMENT REVEALED THAT THE U.S. HAD BEEN IN A RECESSION FOR A YEAR. TO DEAL WITH THE ECONOMY OBAMA CHOSE TIMOTHY GEITHNER (TREASURY SECRETARY), LAWRENCE SUMMERS (NATIONAL ECONOMIC COUNCIL), AND CHRISTINA ROMER (COUNCIL OF ECONOMIC ADVISERS), AS WELL AS TOM DASCHLE (HEALTH AND HUMAN SERVICES SECRETARY). DASCHLE WOULD DROP OUT BEFORE BEING CONFIRMED, OVER TAX ISSUES. GEITHNER ALSO HAD TAX PROBLEMS, BUT WAS FINALLY CONFIRMED.

ON DECEMBER 9, SCANDAL ERUPTED WHEN ILLINOIS GOVERNOR ROD BLAGOJEVICH WAS ARRESTED AFTER BEING ACCUSED OF TRYING TO SELL OBAMA'S VACATED SENATE SEAT. THE LEGISLATURE WOULD IMPEACH HIM IN LATE JANUARY, BUT NOT BEFORE HE APPOINTED ROLAND BURRIS IN THE SENATE.

MORE CABINET CHOICES WERE MADE, INCLUDING THE ENVIRONMENT AND ENERGY TEAM OF STEVEN CHU (ENERGY SECRETARY), CAROL BROWNER (CLIMATE CZAR), AND LISA JACKSON (ENVIRONMENTAL PROTECTION AGENCY).

ALSO NAMED WERE SENATOR KEN SALAZAR (SECRETARY OF THE INTERIOR), TOM VILSACK (INTERIOR SECRETARY), AND ARNE DUNCAN (EDUCATION SECRETARY).

SOME OF HIS CENTRIST CHOICES WERE PRAISED BY THE POLITICAL RIGHT AND FROWNED UPON BY THE LEFT. OBAMA HAD PLEDGED TO GOVERN IN A BIPARTISAN FASHION, AND SEEMED INTENT ON LIVING UP TO THAT PROMISE.

ON JANUARY 5, OBAMA MOVED TO WASHINGTON, DC AND THE GIRLS STARTED SCHOOL AT SIDWELL FRIENDS, A PRIVATE QUAKER SCHOOL. SINCE THE BLAIR HOUSE RESIDENCE WASN'T AVAILABLE YET, THEY WOULD LIVE AT THE HAY-ADAMS HOTEL UNTIL IT WAS.

A FEW DAYS BEFORE HIS INAUGURATION, OBAMA MET WITH MEXICAN PRESIDENT FELIPE CALDERON TO TALK ABOUT CROSS-BORDER ISSUES.

THE BIG DAY WAS ALMOST AT HAND, AND HE WAS READYING HIMSELF FOR IT, WORKING ON HIS INAUGURAL ADDRESS AND PREPARING TO DIVE INTO THE JOB.

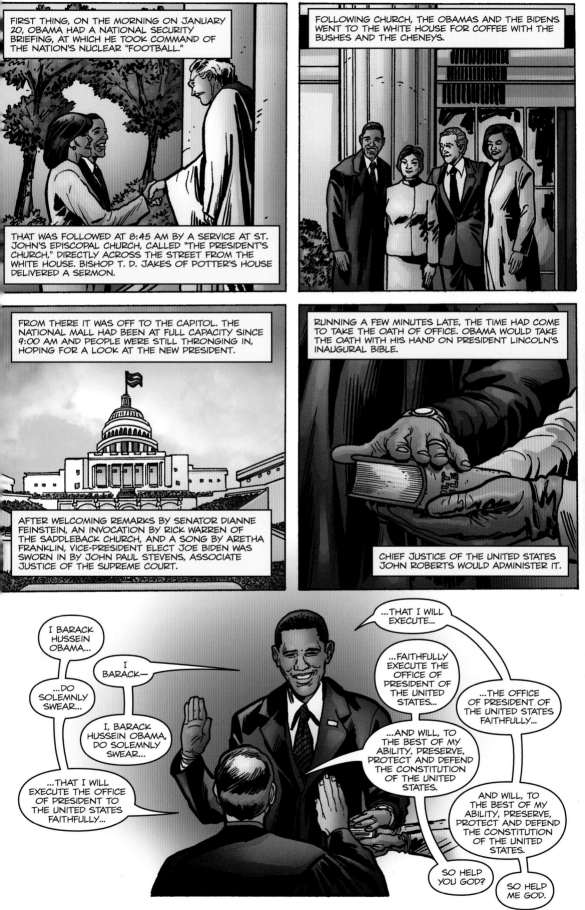

FIRST THING, ON THE MORNING ON JANUARY 20, OBAMA HAD A NATIONAL SECURITY BRIEFING, AT WHICH HE TOOK COMMAND OF THE NATION'S NUCLEAR "FOOTBALL."

THAT WAS FOLLOWED AT 8:45 AM BY A SERVICE AT ST. JOHN'S EPISCOPAL CHURCH, CALLED "THE PRESIDENT'S CHURCH," DIRECTLY ACROSS THE STREET FROM THE WHITE HOUSE. BISHOP T. D. JAKES OF POTTER'S HOUSE DELIVERED A SERMON.

FOLLOWING CHURCH, THE OBAMAS AND THE BIDENS WENT TO THE WHITE HOUSE FOR COFFEE WITH THE BUSHES AND THE CHENEYS.

FROM THERE IT WAS OFF TO THE CAPITOL. THE NATIONAL MALL HAD BEEN AT FULL CAPACITY SINCE 9:00 AM AND PEOPLE WERE STILL THRONGING IN, HOPING FOR A LOOK AT THE NEW PRESIDENT.

AFTER WELCOMING REMARKS BY SENATOR DIANNE FEINSTEIN, AN INVOCATION BY RICK WARREN OF THE SADDLEBACK CHURCH, AND A SONG BY ARETHA FRANKLIN, VICE-PRESIDENT ELECT JOE BIDEN WAS SWORN IN BY JOHN PAUL STEVENS, ASSOCIATE JUSTICE OF THE SUPREME COURT.

RUNNING A FEW MINUTES LATE, THE TIME HAD COME TO TAKE THE OATH OF OFFICE. OBAMA WOULD TAKE THE OATH WITH HIS HAND ON PRESIDENT LINCOLN'S INAUGURAL BIBLE.

CHIEF JUSTICE OF THE UNITED STATES JOHN ROBERTS WOULD ADMINISTER IT.

I BARACK HUSSEIN OBAMA...

I BARACK—

...DO SOLEMNLY SWEAR...

I, BARACK HUSSEIN OBAMA, DO SOLEMNLY SWEAR...

...THAT I WILL EXECUTE THE OFFICE OF PRESIDENT TO THE UNITED STATES FAITHFULLY...

...THAT I WILL EXECUTE...

...FAITHFULLY EXECUTE THE OFFICE OF PRESIDENT OF THE UNITED STATES...

...THE OFFICE OF PRESIDENT OF THE UNITED STATES FAITHFULLY...

...AND WILL, TO THE BEST OF MY ABILITY, PRESERVE, PROTECT AND DEFEND THE CONSTITUTION OF THE UNITED STATES.

AND WILL, TO THE BEST OF MY ABILITY, PRESERVE, PROTECT AND DEFEND THE CONSTITUTION OF THE UNITED STATES.

SO HELP YOU GOD?

SO HELP ME GOD.

TODAY I SAY TO YOU THAT THE CHALLENGES WE FACE ARE REAL. THEY ARE SERIOUS AND THEY ARE MANY. THEY WILL NOT BE MET EASILY OR IN A SHORT SPAN OF TIME. BUT KNOW THIS AMERICA: THEY WILL BE MET.

ON THIS DAY, WE GATHER BECAUSE WE HAVE CHOSEN HOPE OVER FEAR, UNITY OF PURPOSE OVER CONFLICT AND DISCORD.

ON THIS DAY, WE COME TO PROCLAIM AN END TO THE PETTY GRIEVANCES AND FALSE PROMISES, THE RECRIMINATIONS AND WORN-OUT DOGMAS THAT FOR FAR TOO LONG HAVE STRANGLED OUR POLITICS.

WE REMAIN A YOUNG NATION. BUT IN THE WORDS OF SCRIPTURE, THE TIME HAS COME TO SET ASIDE CHILDISH THINGS.

THE TIME HAS COME TO REAFFIRM OUR ENDURING SPIRIT; TO CHOOSE OUR BETTER HISTORY; TO CARRY FORWARD THAT PRECIOUS GIFT, THAT NOBLE IDEA PASSED ON FROM GENERATION TO GENERATION:

THE GOD-GIVEN PROMISE THAT ALL ARE EQUAL, ALL ARE FREE, AND ALL DESERVE A CHANCE TO PURSUE THEIR FULL MEASURE OF HAPPINESS.

NOW, THERE ARE SOME WHO QUESTION THE SCALE OF OUR AMBITIONS, WHO SUGGEST THAT OUR SYSTEM CANNOT TOLERATE TOO MANY BIG PLANS.

THEIR MEMORIES ARE SHORT, FOR THEY HAVE FORGOTTEN WHAT THIS COUNTRY HAS ALREADY DONE, WHAT FREE MEN AND WOMEN CAN ACHIEVE WHEN IMAGINATION IS JOINED TO COMMON PURPOSE, AND NECESSITY TO COURAGE.

WHAT THE CYNICS FAIL TO UNDERSTAND IS THAT THE GROUND HAS SHIFTED BENEATH THEM, THAT THE STALE POLITICAL ARGUMENTS THAT HAVE CONSUMED US FOR SO LONG NO LONGER APPLY.

THE QUESTION WE ASK TODAY IS NOT WHETHER OUR GOVERNMENT IS TOO BIG OR TOO SMALL, BUT WHETHER IT WORKS—

—WHETHER IT HELPS FAMILIES FIND JOBS AT A DECENT WAGE, CARE THEY CAN AFFORD, A RETIREMENT THAT IS DIGNIFIED. WHERE THE ANSWER IS YES, WE INTEND TO MOVE FORWARD.

WHERE THE ANSWER IS NO, PROGRAMS WILL END. AND THOSE OF US WHO MANAGE THE PUBLIC'S DOLLARS WILL BE HELD TO ACCOUNT, TO SPEND WISELY, REFORM BAD HABITS, AND DO OUR BUSINESS IN THE LIGHT OF DAY, BECAUSE ONLY THEN CAN WE RESTORE THE VITAL TRUST BETWEEN A PEOPLE AND THEIR GOVERNMENT.

AS FOR OUR COMMON DEFENSE, WE REJECT AS FALSE THE CHOICE BETWEEN OUR SAFETY AND OUR IDEALS. OUR FOUNDING FATHERS—

—OUR FOUNDING FATHERS, FACED WITH PERILS THAT WE CAN SCARCELY IMAGINE, DRAFTED A CHARTER TO ASSURE THE RULE OF LAW AND THE RIGHTS OF MAN—

—A CHARTER EXPANDED BY THE BLOOD OF GENERATIONS. THOSE IDEALS STILL LIGHT THE WORLD, AND WE WILL NOT GIVE THEM UP FOR EXPEDIENCE SAKE.

AND SO, TO ALL THE OTHER PEOPLES AND GOVERNMENTS WHO ARE WATCHING TODAY, FROM THE GRANDEST CAPITALS TO THE SMALL VILLAGE WHERE MY FATHER WAS BORN, KNOW THAT AMERICA IS A FRIEND OF EACH NATION, AND EVERY MAN, WOMAN AND CHILD WHO SEEKS A FUTURE OF PEACE AND DIGNITY. AND WE ARE READY TO LEAD ONCE MORE.

AMERICA: IN THE FACE OF OUR COMMON DANGERS, IN THIS WINTER OF OUR HARDSHIP, LET US REMEMBER THESE TIMELESS WORDS.

WITH HOPE AND VIRTUE, LET US BRAVE ONCE MORE THE ICY CURRENTS, AND ENDURE WHAT STORMS MAY COME. LET IT BE SAID BY OUR CHILDREN'S CHILDREN THAT WHEN WE WERE TESTED WE REFUSED TO LET THIS JOURNEY END, THAT WE DID NOT TURN BACK NOR DID WE FALTER;

AND WITH EYES FIXED ON THE HORIZON AND GOD'S GRACE UPON US, WE CARRIED FORTH THAT GREAT GIFT OF FREEDOM AND DELIVERED IT SAFELY TO FUTURE GENERATIONS.

THANK YOU. GOD BLESS YOU. AND GOD BLESS THE UNITED STATES OF AMERICA.

THE DAY WAS FULL OF POMP, HISTORY, AND CELEBRATION, AS A NEW FAMILY CAME TO TOWN AND A NEW PRESIDENT MADE HIS FIRST MARKS UPON THE NATION.

IN THE MORNING THE HARD WORK WOULD BEGIN. BUT FOR THE MOMENT... FOR THE MOMENT, THE NEW PRESIDENT AND HIS LOVELY WIFE COULD DANCE.

NEXT: THE FIRST 100 DAYS.

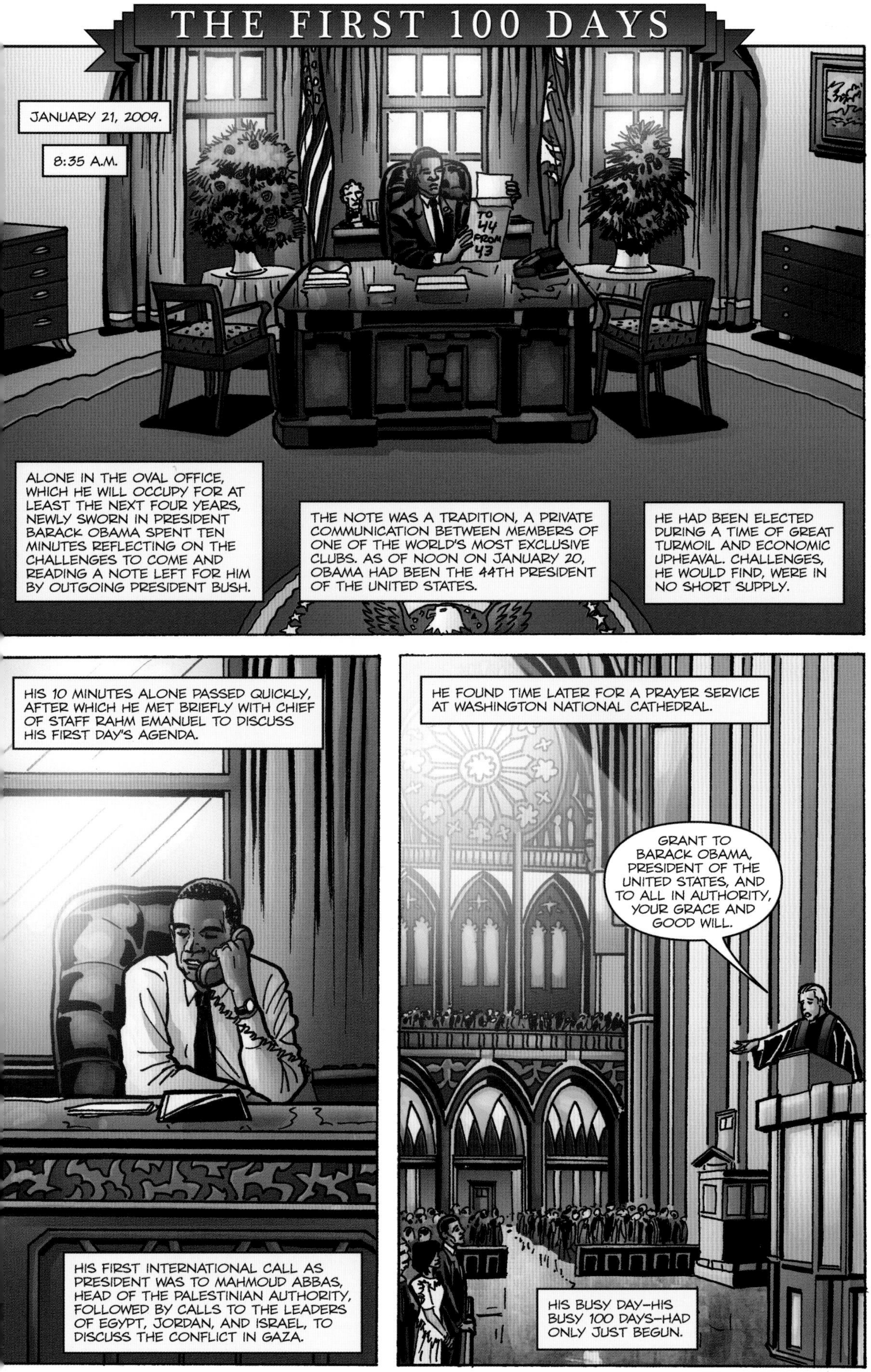
THE FIRST 100 DAYS
JANUARY 21, 2009.
8:35 A.M.
TO 44 FROM 43
ALONE IN THE OVAL OFFICE, WHICH HE WILL OCCUPY FOR AT LEAST THE NEXT FOUR YEARS, NEWLY SWORN IN PRESIDENT BARACK OBAMA SPENT TEN MINUTES REFLECTING ON THE CHALLENGES TO COME AND READING A NOTE LEFT FOR HIM BY OUTGOING PRESIDENT BUSH.
THE NOTE WAS A TRADITION, A PRIVATE COMMUNICATION BETWEEN MEMBERS OF ONE OF THE WORLD'S MOST EXCLUSIVE CLUBS. AS OF NOON ON JANUARY 20, OBAMA HAD BEEN THE 44TH PRESIDENT OF THE UNITED STATES.
HE HAD BEEN ELECTED DURING A TIME OF GREAT TURMOIL AND ECONOMIC UPHEAVAL. CHALLENGES, HE WOULD FIND, WERE IN NO SHORT SUPPLY.
HIS 10 MINUTES ALONE PASSED QUICKLY, AFTER WHICH HE MET BRIEFLY WITH CHIEF OF STAFF RAHM EMANUEL TO DISCUSS HIS FIRST DAY'S AGENDA.
HIS FIRST INTERNATIONAL CALL AS PRESIDENT WAS TO MAHMOUD ABBAS, HEAD OF THE PALESTINIAN AUTHORITY, FOLLOWED BY CALLS TO THE LEADERS OF EGYPT, JORDAN, AND ISRAEL, TO DISCUSS THE CONFLICT IN GAZA.
HE FOUND TIME LATER FOR A PRAYER SERVICE AT WASHINGTON NATIONAL CATHEDRAL.
GRANT TO BARACK OBAMA, PRESIDENT OF THE UNITED STATES, AND TO ALL IN AUTHORITY, YOUR GRACE AND GOOD WILL.
HIS BUSY DAY—HIS BUSY 100 DAYS—HAD ONLY JUST BEGUN.

OBAMA IMMEDIATELY REVERSED SOME BUSH ADMINISTRATION POLICIES, AND THEN ANNOUNCED SOME NEW INITIATIVES, INCLUDING RESTRICTIONS ON GOVERNMENT LOBBYING AND A FREEZE ON THE SALARIES OF TOP WHITE HOUSE AIDES.

HE DIRECTED AGENCIES RESPONDING TO FREEDOM OF INFORMATION ACT REQUESTS TO ERR ON THE SIDE OF INFORMING THE PUBLIC, NOT OF PROTECTING INFORMATION. AND HE FROZE PENDING LAST-MINUTE BUSH REGULATIONS UNTIL HE HAD TIME TO REVIEW THEM.

BARACK AND MICHELLE OBAMA OPENED THE WHITE HOUSE THAT AFTERNOON. NOT ONLY TO CAMPAIGN VOLUNTEERS, BUT TO CURIOUS PEOPLE WHO HAD GATHERED OUTSIDE IN THE BITTER COLD, HOPING FOR A GLIMPSE OF THE NEW FIRST FAMILY.

ENJOY YOURSELF, ROAM AROUND. DON'T BREAK ANYTHING.

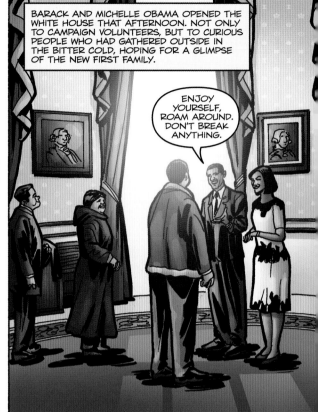

THIS WAS FOLLOWED BY MEETINGS ON TWO MAJOR ISSUES. FIRST HE MET WITH ECONOMIC ADVISORS...

...THEN WITH TOP GENERALS TO DISCUSS THE WAY FORWARD IN IRAQ AND AFGHANISTAN.

AT 7:35, OBAMA CAPPED THE DAY BY RETAKING HIS OATH OF OFFICE, WHICH HAD BEEN FLUBBED AT THE INAUGURATION.

ARE YOU READY TO TAKE THE OATH?

I AM, AND WE'RE GOING TO DO IT VERY SLOWLY.

THIS TIME, THE OATH WENT SMOOTHLY.

THANK YOU, SIR.

CONGRATULATIONS, AGAIN.

WHILE RESPONSIBILITY RESTS ON THE PRESIDENT'S SHOULDERS, IT'S NOT A JOB ONE PERSON CAN DO ALONE. ON JANUARY 21, HILLARY CLINTON WAS CONFIRMED BY THE SENATE AS THE NEW SECRETARY OF STATE. THE VOTE WAS 94-2, A LANDSLIDE VICTORY.

THE SENATE CONFIRMED TIMOTHY GEITHNER, 60-34, AS THE NEW TREASURY SECRETARY ON JANUARY 26. GEITHNER AND CLINTON WOULD HAVE TWO OF THE WORLD'S HARDEST JOBS: TRYING TO FIX A RUPTURED ECONOMY, AND THE COMPLETE REVAMPING OF AMERICA'S FOREIGN POLICY.

OBAMA ANNOUNCED THAT GEORGE MITCHELL WOULD BE HIS MIDDLE EAST ENVOY, AND RICHARD HOLBROOKE A SPECIAL ENVOY TO AFGHANISTAN AND PAKISTAN.

OBAMA'S FIRST INTERVIEW SINCE TAKING OFFICE AIRED ON JANUARY 27, ON AL ARABIYA TV.

MY JOB IS TO COMMUNICATE THE FACT THAT THE UNITED STATES HAS A STAKE IN THE WELL-BEING OF THE MUSLIM WORLD, THAT THE LANGUAGE WE USE HAS TO BE A LANGUAGE OF RESPECT.

THAT SAME DAY, OBAMA WENT TO CAPITOL HILL FOR THE FIRST TIME AS PRESIDENT, TO TRY TO SELL HIS STIMULUS PLAN TO CONGRESSIONAL REPUBLICANS.

TO LITTLE EFFECT... TWO DAYS LATER THE HOUSE WOULD PASS THE $819 BILLION PACKAGE WITHOUT A SINGLE REPUBLICAN VOTE.

NINE DAYS INTO HIS PRESIDENCY, OBAMA SIGNED HIS FIRST BILL, THE LILLY LEDBETTER FAIR PAY ACT. LEDBETTER HAD WORKED AT A JOB FOR ALMOST 20 YEARS BEFORE LEARNING THAT SHE WAS PAID LESS THAN MALE EMPLOYEES FOR THE SAME WORK. EXISTING LAW REQUIRED THAT A DISCRIMINATION CLAIM BE FILED WITHIN 180 DAYS OF AGREEING TO A PAY RATE.

I KNOW THAT IF WE STAY FOCUSED, AS LILLY DID—AND KEEP STANDING FOR WHAT'S RIGHT, AS LILLY DID—WE WILL CLOSE THAT PAY GAP AND WE WILL MAKE SURE THAT OUR DAUGHTERS HAVE THE SAME RIGHTS, THE SAME CHANCES, AND THE SAME FREEDOMS TO PURSUE THEIR DREAMS AS OUR SONS.

THE NEW BILL CHANGED THE STATUTE OF LIMITATIONS TO 180 DAYS AFTER ANY PAYCHECK, SO NO MATTER WHEN SOMEONE DISCOVERED PAY DISCRIMINATION, THEY COULD SPEAK UP.

THE SAME DAY HE STOOD UP FOR WORKING-WOMEN, OBAMA TOOK ON WALL STREET COMPANIES THAT HAD PAID OUT $18 BILLION IN BONUSES WHILE THE ECONOMY CRUMBLED AROUND THEM.

IT IS SHAMEFUL. AND PART OF WHAT WE'RE GOING TO NEED IS FOR THE FOLKS ON WALL STREET WHO ARE ASKING FOR HELP TO SHOW SOME RESTRAINT, AND SHOW SOME DISCIPLINE, AND SHOW SOME SENSE OF RESPONSIBILITY.

ON FEBRUARY 1, DURING THE SUPER BOWL PRE-GAME SHOW, THE PRESIDENT GAVE HIS FIRST DOMESTIC TV INTERVIEW, WITH NBC'S MATT LAUER.

HOW MUCH WORSE IS THE ECONOMY GOING TO GET, MR. PRESIDENT, BEFORE IT GETS BETTER?

WELL, IT—I THINK WE'RE GONNA BE IN FOR A TOUGH SEVERAL MONTHS. WE'VE GOT TO GET THIS ECONOMIC RECOVERY PLAN PASSED. WE'VE GOTTA START PUTTING PEOPLE BACK TO WORK.

WE'RE GONNA HAVE TO STRAIGHTEN OUT THE CREDIT MARKETS AND MAKE SURE THAT CREDIT IS FLOWING TO BUSINESSES AND INDIVIDUALS SO THAT THEY CAN START INVESTING AND HIRING PEOPLE AGAIN.

GIVE ME A SCORE. WHAT'S THE SCORE GONNA BE IN THIS GAME?

YOU KNOW, IT'S—IT'S TOUGH TO PREDICT. BUT I—BUT I THINK THE—THE STEELERS ARE GONNA EKE IT OUT IN A CLOSE ONE.

HE WAS RIGHT. THE STEELERS PULLED OUT A LAST-MINUTE 27-23 VICTORY.

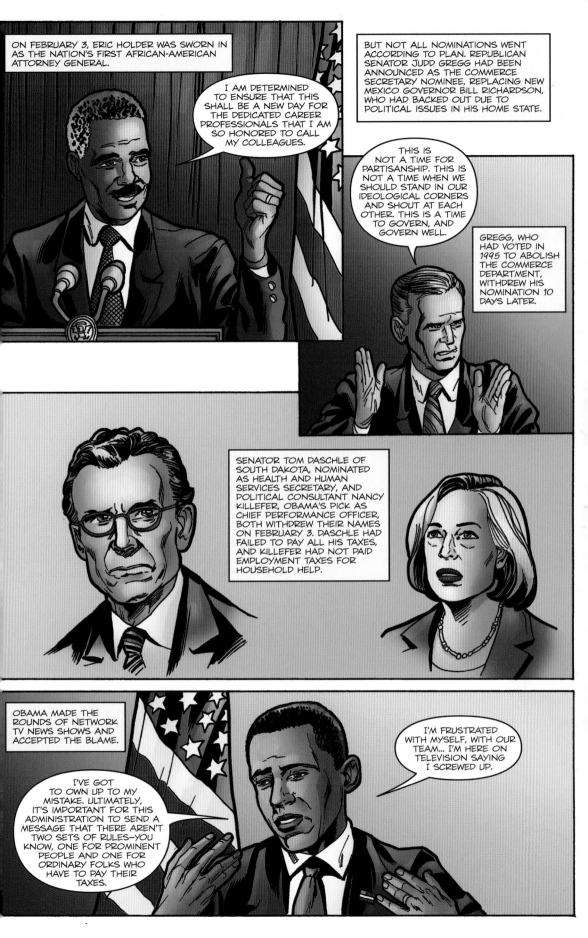

ON FEBRUARY 3, ERIC HOLDER WAS SWORN IN AS THE NATION'S FIRST AFRICAN-AMERICAN ATTORNEY GENERAL.

I AM DETERMINED TO ENSURE THAT THIS SHALL BE A NEW DAY FOR THE DEDICATED CAREER PROFESSIONALS THAT I AM SO HONORED TO CALL MY COLLEAGUES.

BUT NOT ALL NOMINATIONS WENT ACCORDING TO PLAN. REPUBLICAN SENATOR JUDD GREGG HAD BEEN ANNOUNCED AS THE COMMERCE SECRETARY NOMINEE, REPLACING NEW MEXICO GOVERNOR BILL RICHARDSON, WHO HAD BACKED OUT DUE TO POLITICAL ISSUES IN HIS HOME STATE.

THIS IS NOT A TIME FOR PARTISANSHIP. THIS IS NOT A TIME WHEN WE SHOULD STAND IN OUR IDEOLOGICAL CORNERS AND SHOUT AT EACH OTHER. THIS IS A TIME TO GOVERN, AND GOVERN WELL.

GREGG, WHO HAD VOTED IN 1995 TO ABOLISH THE COMMERCE DEPARTMENT, WITHDREW HIS NOMINATION 10 DAYS LATER.

SENATOR TOM DASCHLE OF SOUTH DAKOTA, NOMINATED AS HEALTH AND HUMAN SERVICES SECRETARY, AND POLITICAL CONSULTANT NANCY KILLEFER, OBAMA'S PICK AS CHIEF PERFORMANCE OFFICER, BOTH WITHDREW THEIR NAMES ON FEBRUARY 3. DASCHLE HAD FAILED TO PAY ALL HIS TAXES, AND KILLEFER HAD NOT PAID EMPLOYMENT TAXES FOR HOUSEHOLD HELP.

OBAMA MADE THE ROUNDS OF NETWORK TV NEWS SHOWS AND ACCEPTED THE BLAME.

I'VE GOT TO OWN UP TO MY MISTAKE. ULTIMATELY, IT'S IMPORTANT FOR THIS ADMINISTRATION TO SEND A MESSAGE THAT THERE AREN'T TWO SETS OF RULES—YOU KNOW, ONE FOR PROMINENT PEOPLE AND ONE FOR ORDINARY FOLKS WHO HAVE TO PAY THEIR TAXES.

I'M FRUSTRATED WITH MYSELF, WITH OUR TEAM... I'M HERE ON TELEVISION SAYING I SCREWED UP.

THE OBAMAS SPENT THE WEEKEND OF FEBRUARY 7-8 AT CAMP DAVID, THEIR FIRST VISIT TO THE PRESIDENTIAL RETREAT.

AFTER THAT BRIEF INTERLUDE, THE PRESIDENT WENT ON THE ROAD, PUSHING HIS ECONOMIC RECOVERY PLAN. HIS FIRST STOP WAS A TOWN HALL IN ELKHART, INDIANA, A COMMUNITY THAT HAD NOT VOTED FOR HIM AND WHERE UNEMPLOYMENT, AT 15.3%, WAS THE WORST IN THE COUNTRY.

YOU'VE COME TO OUR COUNTY AND ASKED US TO TRUST YOU, BUT THOSE THAT YOU HAVE APPOINTED TO YOUR CABINET ARE NOT TRUSTWORTHY AND CAN'T HANDLE THEIR OWN BUDGET AND TAXES.

I'M—I'M ONE OF THOSE THAT THINKS YOU NEED TO HAVE A BEER WITH SEAN HANNITY. SO TELL ME WHY, FROM MY SIDE, WE CAN...

THE CROWD BEGAN TO BOO.

THIS IS A PERFECTLY LEGITIMATE QUESTION. FIRST OF ALL, I APPOINT—I'VE APPOINTED HUNDREDS OF PEOPLE, ALL OF WHOM ARE OUTSTANDING AMERICANS WHO ARE DOING A GREAT JOB. THERE ARE A COUPLE WHO HAD PROBLEMS BEFORE THEY CAME INTO MY ADMINISTRATION, IN TERMS OF—IN TERMS OF— IN TERMS OF THEIR TAXES.

NOW, UNDERSTAND, THOUGH, I THINK SOMETHING THAT SHOULD ALSO BE MENTIONED IS THAT WE'VE SET UP AN UNPRECEDENTED SET OF ETHICS RULES IN MY WHITE HOUSE WHERE WE ARE—WE ARE NOT—WE ARE NOT—EVERYBODY WILL ACKNOWLEDGE THAT WE HAVE SET UP THE HIGHEST STANDARD EVER FOR LOBBYISTS NOT WORKING IN THE ADMINISTRATION.

NOW, WITH RESPECT TO SEAN HANNITY, I DIDN'T KNOW THAT HE HAD INVITED ME FOR A BEER. YOU KNOW, BUT—I WILL TAKE THAT UNDER ADVISEMENT. GENERALLY, HIS OPINION OF ME DOES NOT SEEM TO BE VERY HIGH, BUT—BUT I'M ALWAYS GOOD FOR A BEER.

LATER THAT NIGHT, OBAMA GAVE HIS FIRST PRIME TIME PRESS CONFERENCE.

TODAY SENATOR PATRICK LEAHY ANNOUNCED THAT HE WANTS TO SET UP A TRUTH AND RECONCILIATION COMMITTEE TO INVESTIGATE THE MISDEEDS OF THE BUSH ADMINISTRATION.

HE SAID THAT BEFORE YOU TURN THE PAGE, YOU HAVE TO READ THE PAGE FIRST. DO YOU AGREE WITH SUCH A PROPOSAL, AND ARE YOU WILLING TO RULE OUT RIGHT HERE AND NOW ANY PROSECUTION OF BUSH ADMINISTRATION OFFICIALS?

MY ADMINISTRATION IS GOING TO OPERATE IN A WAY THAT LEAVES NO DOUBT THAT WE DO NOT TORTURE, AND THAT WE ABIDE BY THE GENEVA CONVENTIONS, AND THAT WE OBSERVE OUR TRADITIONS OF RULE OF LAW AND DUE PROCESS, AS WE ARE VIGOROUSLY GOING AFTER TERRORISTS THAT CAN DO US HARM.

AND I DON'T THINK THOSE ARE CONTRADICTORY; I THINK THEY ARE POTENTIALLY COMPLEMENTARY.

ON FEBRUARY 10, OBAMA WAS INTRODUCED AT A FT. MYERS, FLORIDA, TOWN HALL BY GOVERNOR CHARLIE CRIST, A REPUBLICAN WHO SUPPORTED THE STIMULUS PLAN. THE FT. MYERS AREA HAD ONE OF THE WORST FORECLOSURE RATES IN THE COUNTRY.

DURING THE EVENT, WORD CAME THAT THE SENATE HAD PASSED THE STIMULUS BILL, 60-38. THE CROWD ERUPTED IN A STANDING OVATION.

A HOMELESS WOMAN MADE NEWS WITH HER PLEA TO THE PRESIDENT.

I HAVE BEEN PRAYING FOR YOU, MR. PRESIDENT. PLEASE HELP ME AND MY FAMILY. WE NEED YOUR HELP. WE ARE HOMELESS AND LIVING OUT OF OUR VAN. PLEASE HELP US.

OBAMA PROMISED THAT A STAFF MEMBER WOULD TALK TO HER AFTER THE EVENT. WITHIN 2 DAYS, THE WIFE OF FLORIDA STATE REPRESENTATIVE NICK THOMPSON HAD PRESENTED HER WITH THE KEYS TO A RENT-FREE HOUSE.

A LOCAL AID ORGANIZATION CLAIMED THAT THE WOMAN WAS BEING DECEITFUL—THAT SHE HAD TURNED DOWN HELP IN THE PAST FEW WEEKS, AND HAD SOLD PROPERTY FOR $47,000 IN 2005.

THE WOMAN REPLIED THAT THE "HELP" SHE WAS OFFERED CAME WITH PRICE TAGS—RENT SHE COULDN'T AFFORD—AND THAT THE MONEY FROM THE SALE WAS LONG GONE, SPENT ON LIVING EXPENSES.

ON FEBRUARY 17, IN DENVER—THE CITY WHERE HE HAD ACCEPTED THE DEMOCRATIC NOMINATION FOR PRESIDENT—OBAMA SIGNED THE AMERICAN RECOVERY AND REINVESTMENT ACT OF 2009, HIS $787 BILLION STIMULUS BILL.

THE ORIGINAL REQUEST HAD BEEN FOR $825 BILLION, BUT THE PRESIDENT GOT MOST OF WHAT HE WANTED IN THE FINAL VERSION.

SECRETARY OF STATE CLINTON LEFT ON FEBRUARY 16 FOR ASIA, HER FIRST FOREIGN TRIP.

SHE WOULD MAKE STOPS IN JAPAN, SOUTH KOREA, INDONESIA AND CHINA.

ON FEBRUARY 19, OBAMA MADE HIS FIRST INTERNATIONAL JOURNEY, ACROSS THE BORDER TO OTTAWA, CANADA—LONG A TRADITIONAL FIRST STOP FOR NEW PRESIDENTS, ALTHOUGH GEORGE BUSH HAD GONE SOUTH OF THE BORDER INSTEAD.

DURING HIS BRIEF VISIT, OBAMA WAS WELCOMED ENTHUSIASTICALLY BY THE CANADIAN PEOPLE—A TREND THAT WOULD CONTINUE ON HIS NEXT OVERSEAS TRIP.

WELCOM OBAMA

YES CAN...ADA

BACK IN WASHINGTON, THE OBAMA FAMILY HAD EMBARKED ON A WHIRLWIND OF ACTIVITY, TRANSFORMING THE WHITE HOUSE INTO THEIR HOME.

THEY HOSTED AN EVENT HONORING STEVIE WONDER, ONE THAT INCLUDED PERFORMANCES BY TONY BENNETT, WILL.I.AM, DIANA KRALL, AND OTHERS.

THE OBAMAS HELD THEIR FIRST FORMAL WHITE HOUSE DINNER FOR THE NATIONAL GOVERNORS ASSOCIATION. *EARTH, WIND AND FIRE* PROVIDED AFTER-DINNER ENTERTAINMENT.

THEY DECLARED WEDNESDAY EVENING COCKTAIL PARTY TIME, HOSTING A WIDE RANGE OF GUESTS, FROM BLUE DOG DEMOCRATS TO THE CONGRESSIONAL BLACK CAUCUS TO THE HEADS OF PROGRESSIVE GROUPS LIKE MOVEON, THE SIERRA CLUB, AND THE HUMAN RIGHTS CAMPAIGN.

THE WHITE HOUSE SEEMED LIVELIER THAN IT HAD ANYTIME SINCE THE REAGAN ADMINISTRATION, AND COMPARISONS TO CAMELOT WERE INEVITABLE.

BUT THE FIRST COUPLE DID NOT JUST STAY HOME, THEY SAMPLED LOCAL WASHINGTON RESTAURANTS ON A REGULAR BASIS.

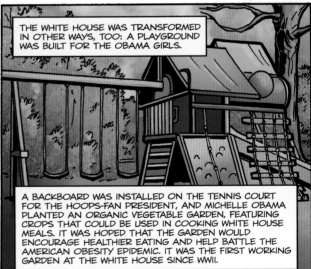

THE WHITE HOUSE WAS TRANSFORMED IN OTHER WAYS, TOO: A PLAYGROUND WAS BUILT FOR THE OBAMA GIRLS.

A BACKBOARD WAS INSTALLED ON THE TENNIS COURT FOR THE HOOPS-FAN PRESIDENT, AND MICHELLE OBAMA PLANTED AN ORGANIC VEGETABLE GARDEN, FEATURING CROPS THAT COULD BE USED IN COOKING WHITE HOUSE MEALS. IT WAS HOPED THAT THE GARDEN WOULD ENCOURAGE HEALTHIER EATING AND HELP BATTLE THE AMERICAN OBESITY EPIDEMIC. IT WAS THE FIRST WORKING GARDEN AT THE WHITE HOUSE SINCE WWII.

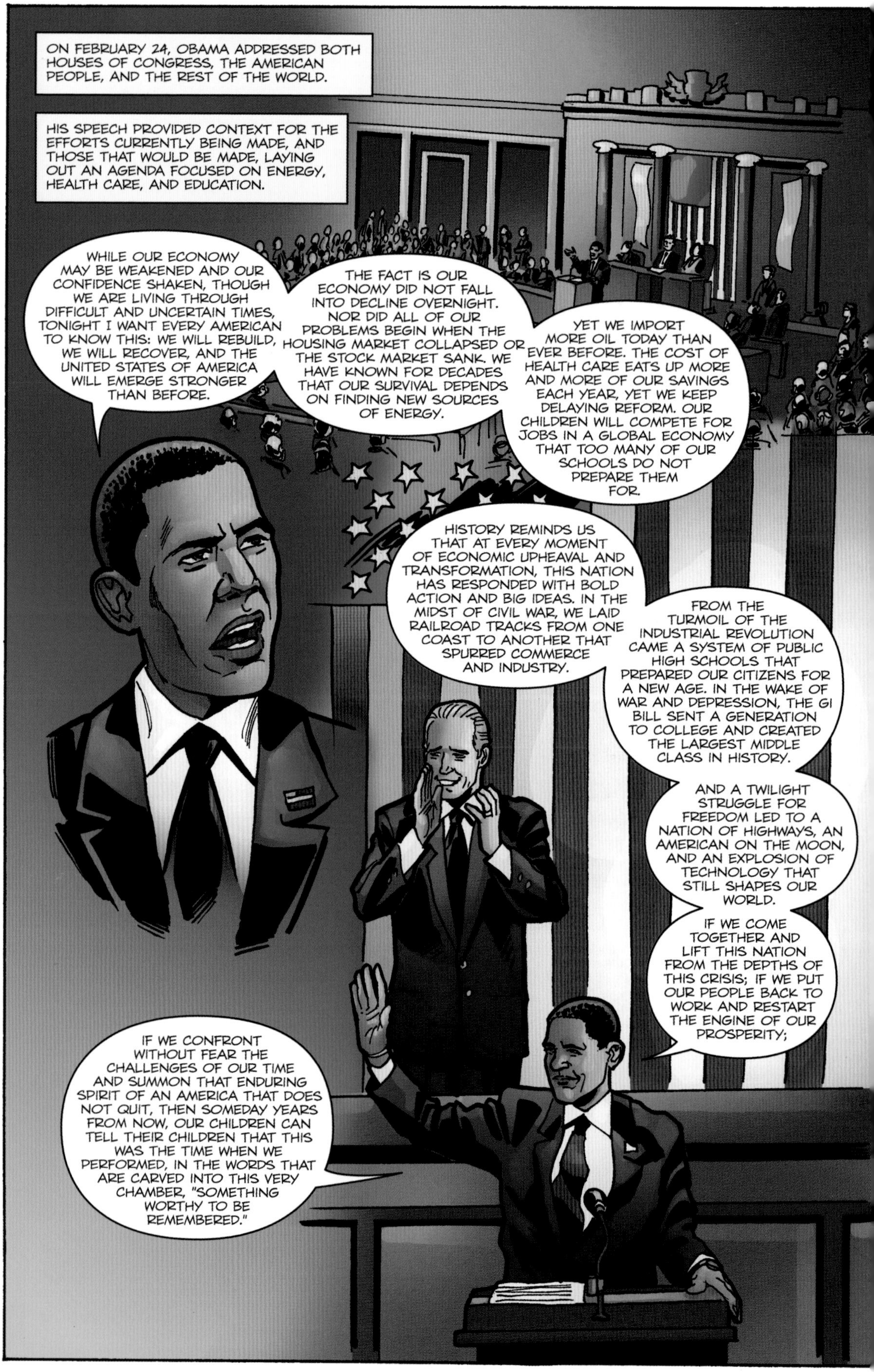
ON FEBRUARY 24, OBAMA ADDRESSED BOTH HOUSES OF CONGRESS, THE AMERICAN PEOPLE, AND THE REST OF THE WORLD.
HIS SPEECH PROVIDED CONTEXT FOR THE EFFORTS CURRENTLY BEING MADE, AND THOSE THAT WOULD BE MADE, LAYING OUT AN AGENDA FOCUSED ON ENERGY, HEALTH CARE, AND EDUCATION.
WHILE OUR ECONOMY MAY BE WEAKENED AND OUR CONFIDENCE SHAKEN, THOUGH WE ARE LIVING THROUGH DIFFICULT AND UNCERTAIN TIMES, TONIGHT I WANT EVERY AMERICAN TO KNOW THIS: WE WILL REBUILD, WE WILL RECOVER, AND THE UNITED STATES OF AMERICA WILL EMERGE STRONGER THAN BEFORE.
THE FACT IS OUR ECONOMY DID NOT FALL INTO DECLINE OVERNIGHT. NOR DID ALL OF OUR PROBLEMS BEGIN WHEN THE HOUSING MARKET COLLAPSED OR THE STOCK MARKET SANK. WE HAVE KNOWN FOR DECADES THAT OUR SURVIVAL DEPENDS ON FINDING NEW SOURCES OF ENERGY.
YET WE IMPORT MORE OIL TODAY THAN EVER BEFORE. THE COST OF HEALTH CARE EATS UP MORE AND MORE OF OUR SAVINGS EACH YEAR, YET WE KEEP DELAYING REFORM. OUR CHILDREN WILL COMPETE FOR JOBS IN A GLOBAL ECONOMY THAT TOO MANY OF OUR SCHOOLS DO NOT PREPARE THEM FOR.
HISTORY REMINDS US THAT AT EVERY MOMENT OF ECONOMIC UPHEAVAL AND TRANSFORMATION, THIS NATION HAS RESPONDED WITH BOLD ACTION AND BIG IDEAS. IN THE MIDST OF CIVIL WAR, WE LAID RAILROAD TRACKS FROM ONE COAST TO ANOTHER THAT SPURRED COMMERCE AND INDUSTRY.
FROM THE TURMOIL OF THE INDUSTRIAL REVOLUTION CAME A SYSTEM OF PUBLIC HIGH SCHOOLS THAT PREPARED OUR CITIZENS FOR A NEW AGE. IN THE WAKE OF WAR AND DEPRESSION, THE GI BILL SENT A GENERATION TO COLLEGE AND CREATED THE LARGEST MIDDLE CLASS IN HISTORY.
AND A TWILIGHT STRUGGLE FOR FREEDOM LED TO A NATION OF HIGHWAYS, AN AMERICAN ON THE MOON, AND AN EXPLOSION OF TECHNOLOGY THAT STILL SHAPES OUR WORLD.
IF WE COME TOGETHER AND LIFT THIS NATION FROM THE DEPTHS OF THIS CRISIS; IF WE PUT OUR PEOPLE BACK TO WORK AND RESTART THE ENGINE OF OUR PROSPERITY;
IF WE CONFRONT WITHOUT FEAR THE CHALLENGES OF OUR TIME AND SUMMON THAT ENDURING SPIRIT OF AN AMERICA THAT DOES NOT QUIT, THEN SOMEDAY YEARS FROM NOW, OUR CHILDREN CAN TELL THEIR CHILDREN THAT THIS WAS THE TIME WHEN WE PERFORMED, IN THE WORDS THAT ARE CARVED INTO THIS VERY CHAMBER, "SOMETHING WORTHY TO BE REMEMBERED."

A CNN POLL FOUND THAT 92% OF VIEWERS HAD A VERY OR SOMEWHAT FAVORABLE RESPONSE TO THE SPEECH, WITH ONLY 8% REPORTING A NEGATIVE RESPONSE. 85% SAID IT MADE THEM FEEL MORE OPTIMISTIC ABOUT THE COUNTRY'S FUTURE.

THE NEXT DAY OBAMA ANNOUNCED YET ANOTHER PICK FOR COMMERCE SECRETARY, DEMOCRAT GARY LOCKE. ON FEBRUARY 26, HE SUBMITTED A $4 TRILLION BUDGET PROPOSAL, THE LARGEST IN HISTORY, TO MOVE HIS PLAN FROM RHETORIC TO REALITY.

REPUBLICANS AND BLUE DOG DEMOCRATS ALIKE OBJECTED TO THE PROPOSAL'S SIZE AND SCOPE.

DESPITE OPPOSITION, THE BUDGET, ONLY SLIGHTLY REDUCED, PASSED THE HOUSE AND SENATE ON APRIL 3, WITHOUT GARNERING A SINGLE REPUBLICAN VOTE IN EITHER CHAMBER.

OBAMA KEPT MAKING NEWS, VISITING MARINE BASE CAMP LEJEUNE THE FOLLOWING DAY TO DELIVER ANOTHER MAJOR ANNOUNCEMENT.

TODAY, I HAVE COME TO SPEAK TO YOU ABOUT HOW THE WAR IN IRAQ WILL END.

AS A CANDIDATE FOR PRESIDENT, I MADE CLEAR MY SUPPORT FOR A TIMELINE OF 16 MONTHS TO CARRY OUT THIS DRAWDOWN, WHILE PLEDGING TO CONSULT CLOSELY WITH OUR MILITARY COMMANDERS UPON TAKING OFFICE TO ENSURE THAT WE PRESERVE THE GAINS WE'VE MADE AND PROTECT OUR TROOPS.

THOSE CONSULTATIONS ARE NOW COMPLETE, AND I HAVE CHOSEN A TIMELINE THAT WILL REMOVE OUR COMBAT BRIGADES OVER THE NEXT 18 MONTHS.

LET ME SAY THIS AS PLAINLY AS I CAN: BY AUGUST 31, 2010, OUR COMBAT MISSION IN IRAQ WILL END.

OBAMA STARTED HIS PUSH ON HEALTH CARE BY CONVENING A SUMMIT AT THE WHITE HOUSE, BRINGING TOGETHER MEMBERS OF CONGRESS, INSURANCE EXECUTIVES, HOSPITAL REPRESENTATIVES, LABOR UNIONS, CONSUMER GROUPS, AND MORE.

HEALTH CARE REFORM IS NO LONGER JUST A MORAL IMPERATIVE, IT IS A FISCAL IMPERATIVE. IF WE WANT TO CREATE JOBS, REBUILD OUR ECONOMY, AND GET OUR FEDERAL BUDGET UNDER CONTROL, THEN WE MUST ADDRESS THE CRUSHING COST OF HEALTH CARE THIS YEAR.

HIS NEXT STOP WAS COLUMBUS, OHIO, WHERE HE MET WITH POLICE OFFICERS WHOSE JOBS HAD BEEN PRESERVED BY THE STIMULUS BILL.

WHILE HE WAS ON THE ROAD, PROMOTING THE BENEFITS OF A BILL THAT HAD ALREADY BEEN SIGNED, CONGRESS WRESTLED WITH A STOPGAP BUDGET MEASURE TO KEEP THE GOVERNMENT FROM SHUTTING DOWN WHILE THE NEW BUDGET PROPOSAL WORKED ITS WAY THROUGH THE SLOW LEGISLATIVE PROCESS.

ON MARCH 9, THE PRESIDENT KEPT A CAMPAIGN PROMISE BY LIFTING THE BUSH-ERA BAN ON FUNDING FOR STEM CELL RESEARCH.

BUT WHILE THE SCIENTIFIC COMMUNITY REJOICED AT THAT NEWS, THE FINANCIAL COMMUNITY HAD AN ENTIRELY DIFFERENT REACTION TO TREASURY SECRETARY GEITHNER'S ANNOUNCEMENT THAT HIS DETAILED PLAN FOR AN OVERHAUL OF THE FINANCIAL REGULATORY SYSTEM WOULD BE DELAYED.

THE STOCK MARKET PLUMMETED THAT DAY.

OBAMA SIGNED A $410 BILLION APPROPRIATIONS BILL ON MARCH 11. THE BILL HAD BEEN DRAFTED IN THE FALL, BY THE PREVIOUS ADMINISTRATION, AND CONGRESS HAD DELAYED IT UNTIL AFTER THE CHANGE IN POWER.

HE CALLED THE LEGISLATION "IMPERFECT," AND DECLARING PARTS OF IT UNCONSTITUTIONAL, ISSUED THE FIRST SIGNING STATEMENT OF HIS PRESIDENCY, RESERVING THE RIGHT TO IGNORE SOME OF ITS PROVISIONS.

MICHELLE OBAMA MADE HER FIRST OFFICIAL TRIP AS FIRST LADY TO FT. BRAGG, NORTH CAROLINA, TO RAISE ATTENTION TO THE SITUATION OF SERVICE MEMBERS' FAMILIES LEFT BEHIND BY DEPLOYED SOLDIERS.

OUR SOLDIERS AND THEIR FAMILIES HAVE DONE THEIR DUTY— AND THEY DO IT WITHOUT COMPLAINT. AND WE AS A GRATEFUL NATION MUST DO OURS—DO EVERYTHING IN OUR POWER TO HONOR THEM BY SUPPORTING THEM.

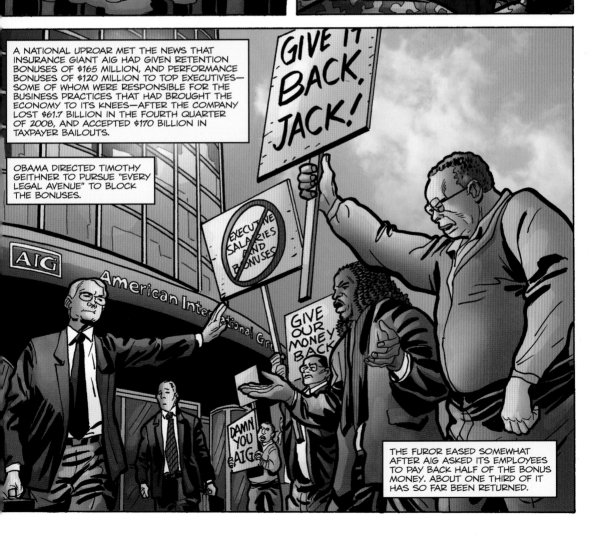

A NATIONAL UPROAR MET THE NEWS THAT INSURANCE GIANT AIG HAD GIVEN RETENTION BONUSES OF $165 MILLION, AND PERFORMANCE BONUSES OF $120 MILLION TO TOP EXECUTIVES— SOME OF WHOM WERE RESPONSIBLE FOR THE BUSINESS PRACTICES THAT HAD BROUGHT THE ECONOMY TO ITS KNEES—AFTER THE COMPANY LOST $61.7 BILLION IN THE FOURTH QUARTER OF 2008, AND ACCEPTED $170 BILLION IN TAXPAYER BAILOUTS.

OBAMA DIRECTED TIMOTHY GEITHNER TO PURSUE "EVERY LEGAL AVENUE" TO BLOCK THE BONUSES.

GIVE IT BACK, JACK!

EXECUTIVE SALARIES AND BONUSES

AIG

American International Group

GIVE OUR MONEY BACK

DAMN YOU AIG

THE FUROR EASED SOMEWHAT AFTER AIG ASKED ITS EMPLOYEES TO PAY BACK HALF OF THE BONUS MONEY. ABOUT ONE THIRD OF IT HAS SO FAR BEEN RETURNED.

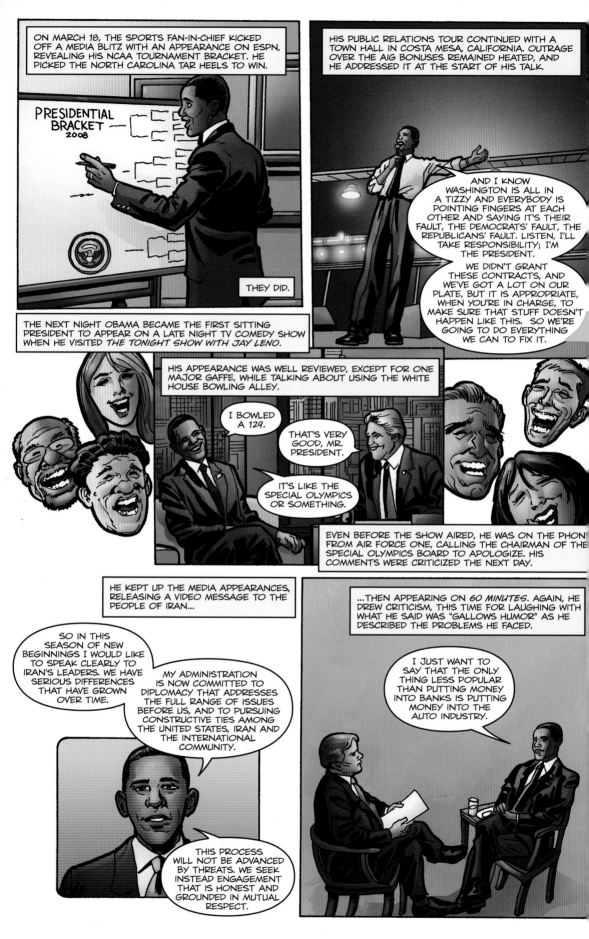

ON MARCH 18, THE SPORTS FAN-IN-CHIEF KICKED OFF A MEDIA BLITZ WITH AN APPEARANCE ON ESPN, REVEALING HIS NCAA TOURNAMENT BRACKET. HE PICKED THE NORTH CAROLINA TAR HEELS TO WIN.

PRESIDENTIAL BRACKET 2008

THEY DID.

HIS PUBLIC RELATIONS TOUR CONTINUED WITH A TOWN HALL IN COSTA MESA, CALIFORNIA. OUTRAGE OVER THE AIG BONUSES REMAINED HEATED, AND HE ADDRESSED IT AT THE START OF HIS TALK.

AND I KNOW WASHINGTON IS ALL IN A TIZZY AND EVERYBODY IS POINTING FINGERS AT EACH OTHER AND SAYING IT'S THEIR FAULT, THE DEMOCRATS' FAULT, THE REPUBLICANS' FAULT. LISTEN, I'LL TAKE RESPONSIBILITY; I'M THE PRESIDENT.

WE DIDN'T GRANT THESE CONTRACTS, AND WE'VE GOT A LOT ON OUR PLATE, BUT IT IS APPROPRIATE, WHEN YOU'RE IN CHARGE, TO MAKE SURE THAT STUFF DOESN'T HAPPEN LIKE THIS. SO WE'RE GOING TO DO EVERYTHING WE CAN TO FIX IT.

THE NEXT NIGHT OBAMA BECAME THE FIRST SITTING PRESIDENT TO APPEAR ON A LATE NIGHT TV COMEDY SHOW WHEN HE VISITED THE TONIGHT SHOW WITH JAY LENO.

HIS APPEARANCE WAS WELL REVIEWED, EXCEPT FOR ONE MAJOR GAFFE, WHILE TALKING ABOUT USING THE WHITE HOUSE BOWLING ALLEY.

I BOWLED A 129.

THAT'S VERY GOOD, MR. PRESIDENT.

IT'S LIKE THE SPECIAL OLYMPICS OR SOMETHING.

EVEN BEFORE THE SHOW AIRED, HE WAS ON THE PHONE FROM AIR FORCE ONE, CALLING THE CHAIRMAN OF THE SPECIAL OLYMPICS BOARD TO APOLOGIZE. HIS COMMENTS WERE CRITICIZED THE NEXT DAY.

HE KEPT UP THE MEDIA APPEARANCES, RELEASING A VIDEO MESSAGE TO THE PEOPLE OF IRAN...

SO IN THIS SEASON OF NEW BEGINNINGS I WOULD LIKE TO SPEAK CLEARLY TO IRAN'S LEADERS. WE HAVE SERIOUS DIFFERENCES THAT HAVE GROWN OVER TIME.

MY ADMINISTRATION IS NOW COMMITTED TO DIPLOMACY THAT ADDRESSES THE FULL RANGE OF ISSUES BEFORE US, AND TO PURSUING CONSTRUCTIVE TIES AMONG THE UNITED STATES, IRAN AND THE INTERNATIONAL COMMUNITY.

THIS PROCESS WILL NOT BE ADVANCED BY THREATS. WE SEEK INSTEAD ENGAGEMENT THAT IS HONEST AND GROUNDED IN MUTUAL RESPECT.

...THEN APPEARING ON 60 MINUTES. AGAIN, HE DREW CRITICISM, THIS TIME FOR LAUGHING WITH WHAT HE SAID WAS "GALLOWS HUMOR" AS HE DESCRIBED THE PROBLEMS HE FACED.

I JUST WANT TO SAY THAT THE ONLY THING LESS POPULAR THAN PUTTING MONEY INTO BANKS IS PUTTING MONEY INTO THE AUTO INDUSTRY.

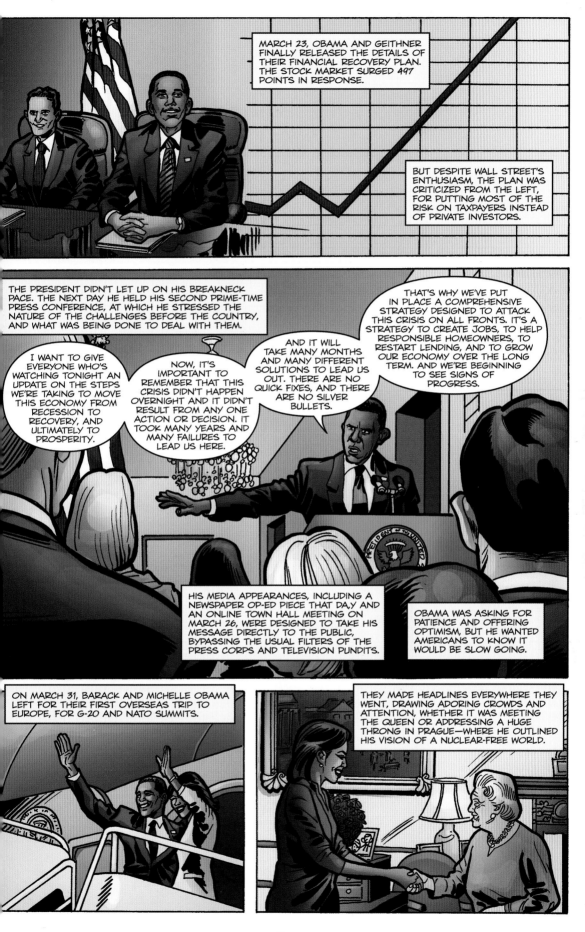

MARCH 23, OBAMA AND GEITHNER FINALLY RELEASED THE DETAILS OF THEIR FINANCIAL RECOVERY PLAN. THE STOCK MARKET SURGED 497 POINTS IN RESPONSE.

BUT DESPITE WALL STREET'S ENTHUSIASM, THE PLAN WAS CRITICIZED FROM THE LEFT, FOR PUTTING MOST OF THE RISK ON TAXPAYERS INSTEAD OF PRIVATE INVESTORS.

THE PRESIDENT DIDN'T LET UP ON HIS BREAKNECK PACE. THE NEXT DAY HE HELD HIS SECOND PRIME-TIME PRESS CONFERENCE, AT WHICH HE STRESSED THE NATURE OF THE CHALLENGES BEFORE THE COUNTRY, AND WHAT WAS BEING DONE TO DEAL WITH THEM.

I WANT TO GIVE EVERYONE WHO'S WATCHING TONIGHT AN UPDATE ON THE STEPS WE'RE TAKING TO MOVE THIS ECONOMY FROM RECESSION TO RECOVERY, AND ULTIMATELY TO PROSPERITY.

NOW, IT'S IMPORTANT TO REMEMBER THAT THIS CRISIS DIDN'T HAPPEN OVERNIGHT AND IT DIDN'T RESULT FROM ANY ONE ACTION OR DECISION. IT TOOK MANY YEARS AND MANY FAILURES TO LEAD US HERE.

AND IT WILL TAKE MANY MONTHS AND MANY DIFFERENT SOLUTIONS TO LEAD US OUT. THERE ARE NO QUICK FIXES, AND THERE ARE NO SILVER BULLETS.

THAT'S WHY WE'VE PUT IN PLACE A COMPREHENSIVE STRATEGY DESIGNED TO ATTACK THIS CRISIS ON ALL FRONTS. IT'S A STRATEGY TO CREATE JOBS, TO HELP RESPONSIBLE HOMEOWNERS, TO RESTART LENDING, AND TO GROW OUR ECONOMY OVER THE LONG TERM. AND WE'RE BEGINNING TO SEE SIGNS OF PROGRESS.

HIS MEDIA APPEARANCES, INCLUDING A NEWSPAPER OP-ED PIECE THAT DAY AND AN ONLINE TOWN HALL MEETING ON MARCH 26, WERE DESIGNED TO TAKE HIS MESSAGE DIRECTLY TO THE PUBLIC, BYPASSING THE USUAL FILTERS OF THE PRESS CORPS AND TELEVISION PUNDITS.

OBAMA WAS ASKING FOR PATIENCE AND OFFERING OPTIMISM, BUT HE WANTED AMERICANS TO KNOW IT WOULD BE SLOW GOING.

ON MARCH 31, BARACK AND MICHELLE OBAMA LEFT FOR THEIR FIRST OVERSEAS TRIP TO EUROPE, FOR G-20 AND NATO SUMMITS.

THEY MADE HEADLINES EVERYWHERE THEY WENT, DRAWING ADORING CROWDS AND ATTENTION, WHETHER IT WAS MEETING THE QUEEN OR ADDRESSING A HUGE THRONG IN PRAGUE—WHERE HE OUTLINED HIS VISION OF A NUCLEAR-FREE WORLD.

IN LONDON, THE NEW AMERICAN PRESIDENT HAD TO PLAY PEACEMAKER WHEN A STANDOFF BETWEEN FRENCH PRESIDENT NICHOLAS SARKOZY AND CHINESE PRESIDENT HU JINTAO THREATENED TO DERAIL THE G-20 SUMMIT.

HE TOOK THEM ASIDE AND SPOKE PRIVATELY TO EACH, AND THEN BROUGHT THEM TOGETHER AND THEY HAMMERED OUT AN AGREEMENT.

AFTER ARRIVING IN STRASBOURG FOR THE NATO SUMMIT, OBAMA FOUND HIMSELF INTERVENING AGAIN, THIS TIME BRINGING A RESOLUTION TO A DISPUTE BETWEEN TURKEY AND DENMARK.

HE DIDN'T GET ALL THE CONCESSIONS HE WANTED AT EITHER SUMMIT, BUT HE MADE IT CLEAR THAT HIS WOULD BE A NEW KIND OF FOREIGN POLICY, STRESSING DIPLOMACY AND COOPERATION.

WHILE HE WAS OVERSEAS, NORTH KOREA TEST FIRED A LONG-RANGE ROCKET. THE LAUNCH WAS WIDELY CONSIDERED A FAILURE ALTHOUGH THE NORTH KOREANS CLAIMED TO HAVE PUT A SATELLITE IN ORBIT.

OBAMA'S NEXT STOP WAS IN TURKEY—HIS FIRST PRESIDENTIAL VISIT TO A MUSLIM NATION. THERE, SPEAKING BEFORE THE TURKISH PARLIAMENT, HE MADE AN APPEAL TO THE MUSLIM WORLD.

LET ME SAY THIS AS CLEARLY AS I CAN: THE UNITED STATES IS NOT AND WILL NEVER BE AT WAR WITH ISLAM. IN FACT, OUR PARTNERSHIP WITH THE MUSLIM WORLD IS CRITICAL IN ROLLING BACK A FRINGE IDEOLOGY THAT PEOPLE OF ALL FAITHS REJECT.

HE CAPPED OFF THAT PART OF THE TRIP WITH A TOWN HALL MEETING FOR TURKISH STUDENTS, MUCH AS HE HAD DONE FOR FRENCH AND GERMAN STUDENTS BEFORE LEAVING STRASBOURG.

I BELIEVE WE CAN HAVE A DIALOGUE THAT'S OPEN, HONEST, VIBRANT AND GROUNDED IN RESPECT. AND I WANT YOU TO KNOW THAT I'M PERSONALLY COMMITTED TO A NEW CHAPTER OF AMERICAN ENGAGEMENT.

WE CAN'T AFFORD TO TALK PAST ONE ANOTHER, TO FOCUS ONLY ON OUR DIFFERENCES OR TO LET THE WALLS OF MISTRUST GO UP AROUND US. INSTEAD, WE HAVE TO LISTEN CAREFULLY TO EACH OTHER.

WE HAVE TO FOCUS ON PLACES WHERE WE CAN FIND COMMON GROUND AND RESPECT EACH OTHER'S VIEWS, EVEN WHEN WE DISAGREE. AND IF WE DO SO, I BELIEVE WE CAN BRIDGE SOME OF OUR DIFFERENCES AND DIVISIONS THAT WE'VE HAD IN THE PAST.

INSTEAD OF HEADING HOME AFTER THAT, THE PRESIDENT MADE AN UNANNOUNCED VISIT TO IRAQ.

IN BAGHDAD HE MET VERY ENTHUSIASTIC TROOPS. HE TOLD THEM THAT THEY HAD PERFORMED BRILLIANTLY AND THE TIME HAD COME FOR THE IRAQIS TO TAKE RESPONSIBILITY FOR THEIR OWN COUNTRY.

DURING HIS SHORT VISIT, HE MET WITH IRAQI PRIME MINISTER NOURI AL-MALIKI, AS WELL AS U.S. GENERAL RAY ODIERNO, TALKING OVER PLANS FOR THE PROJECTED 19-MONTH DRAWDOWN OF TROOPS THERE.

FINALLY HOME AGAIN, OBAMA BECAME THE FIRST SITTING PRESIDENT TO HOST A PASSOVER SEDER AT THE WHITE HOUSE.

EVERYWHERE OBAMA HAD TRAVELED SINCE WINNING THE WHITE HOUSE HE FACED THE SAME QUESTION—WHEN DO THE GIRLS GET THEIR DOG?

BO, A PORTUGUESE WATER DOG, A GIFT FROM SENATOR TED KENNEDY, ARRIVED AT THE WHITE HOUSE ON APRIL 11, AND WAS OFFICIALLY INTRODUCED TO THE NATION ON APRIL 13.

EASTER SUNDAY BEGAN WITH CHURCH SERVICES AT ST. JOHN'S EPISCOPAL CHURCH. LATER, A RECORD 30,000 VISITORS ATTENDED THE ANNUAL WHITE HOUSE EASTER EGG ROLL.

OBAMA HAD PROMISED TO RESCUE A SHELTER DOG, BUT BO CAME FROM A KENNEL. ACKNOWLEDGING THE DIFFERENCE, THE OBAMAS MADE A DONATION TO THE WASHINGTON HUMANE SOCIETY INSTEAD.

THE PRESIDENT'S DRAMATIC READING OF MAURICE SENDAK'S CLASSIC *WHERE THE WILD THINGS ARE* WAS SO CONVINCING THAT AT LEAST ONE CHILD BROKE OUT IN FRIGHTENED TEARS.

THESE WILD THINGS CAN BE A LITTLE SCARY.

IN THE OUTSIDE WORLD, A TERRIFYING SITUATION WAS BROUGHT TO A BLOODY CLOSE WHEN NAVY SNIPERS, ACTING UNDER OBAMA'S ORDERS, KILLED THREE PIRATES HOLDING AMERICAN SHIP CAPTAIN RICHARD PHILLIPS HOSTAGE.

A FOURTH PIRATE WAS ARRESTED AND BROUGHT TO THE U.S. FOR TRIAL. PHILLIPS HAD BEEN HELD OFF THE HORN OF AFRICA FOR FIVE DAYS.

ON APRIL 14, OBAMA GAVE A MAJOR SPEECH IN WHICH HE TIED REFORMS IN EDUCATION, HEALTH CARE, AND ENERGY TO ECONOMIC RECOVERY.

IN IT HE ADDRESSED CRITICISMS OF TRYING TO DO TOO MUCH, OR TOO LITTLE, OR THAT HE WAS BEING NAIVELY OPTIMISTIC ABOUT THE FUTURE. THE PRESIDENT EXPLAINED IN CLEAR LANGUAGE HOW THE RECESSION STARTED, AND OUTLINED HIS VISION OF ITS END.

THERE IS A PARABLE AT THE END OF THE SERMON ON THE MOUNT THAT TELLS THE STORY OF TWO MEN. THE FIRST BUILT HIS HOUSE ON A PILE OF SAND, AND IT WAS DESTROYED AS SOON AS THE STORM HIT.

BUT THE SECOND IS KNOWN AS THE WISE MAN, FOR WHEN "...THE RAIN DESCENDED, AND THE FLOODS CAME, AND THE WINDS BLEW, AND BEAT UPON THAT HOUSE... IT FELL NOT: FOR IT WAS FOUNDED UPON A ROCK."

WE CANNOT REBUILD THIS ECONOMY ON THE SAME PILE OF SAND. WE MUST BUILD OUR HOUSE UPON A ROCK. WE MUST LAY A NEW FOUNDATION FOR GROWTH AND PROSPERITY—A FOUNDATION THAT WILL MOVE US FROM AN ERA OF BORROW AND SPEND TO ONE WHERE WE SAVE AND INVEST, WHERE WE CONSUME LESS AT HOME AND SEND MORE EXPORTS ABROAD.

THE NEXT DAY WAS APRIL 15: TAX DAY. OBAMA'S SPEECH, AND HIS ALREADY-IN-EFFECT TAX CUTS FOR 95% OF AMERICANS, HAD LITTLE IMPACT ON THOSE WHO GATHERED AT "TEA PARTIES" ACROSS THE COUNTRY TO PROTEST WHAT THEY CONSIDERED HIGH TAXES, SPIRALING DEFICITS, AND RUNAWAY GOVERNMENT SPENDING.

Give Me Liberty... NOT DEBT!

ON APRIL 16, HE LEFT FOR ANOTHER INTERNATIONAL TRIP, TO MEXICO AND THEN TRINIDAD AND TOBAGO FOR A SUMMIT OF THE AMERICAS.

DURING A SHORT STAY IN MEXICO, HE DISCUSSED THE RISING TIDE OF DRUG VIOLENCE WITH PRESIDENT FELIPE CALDERON.

A HANDSHAKE BETWEEN OBAMA AND LEFTIST VENEZUELAN PRESIDENT HUGO CHAVEZ AT THE SUMMIT OF THE AMERICAS BECAME THE GROUNDS FOR AN AVALANCHE OF CRITICISM FROM THE RIGHT.

LESS NOTICED WAS WHAT APPEARED TO BE A STERN TALKING-TO THAT OBAMA GAVE CHAVEZ, CAUGHT ON VIDEO LATER IN THE CONFERENCE.

OBABA RETURNED HOME TO A FIRESTORM OF CONTROVERSY OVER BUSH-ERA "TORTURE MEMOS" HIS ADMINISTRATION HAD RELEASED.

THE MEMOS DESCRIBED "ENHANCED INTERROGATION" TECHNIQUES THE CIA USED ON CERTAIN PRISONERS, INCLUDING WATERBOARDING, STRIKING, CONFINING IN BOXES, SLAMMING INTO WALLS, AND MORE.

THE NEW PRESIDENT HAD ALREADY PROHIBITED THESE TECHNIQUES. NOW HE ADDED THAT CIA OFFICERS WOULD NOT BE PROSECUTED FOR ACTS THEY COMMITTED UNDER ORDERS.

BUT OBAMA HAD TO BACKTRACK SHORTLY AFTER, SINCE PROSECUTING CRIMES IS UP TO THE JUSTICE DEPARTMENT, NOT THE PRESIDENT. BUT HE SPOKE OF THE NECESSITY OF LOOKING FORWARD, NOT BACK, AND ATTORNEY GENERAL ERIC HOLDER ECHOED OBAMA'S VIEW OF TORTURE PROSECUTIONS.

THE TOPIC DOMINATED WASHINGTON FOR WEEKS, SPURRED ON BY THE RELEASE OF MORE DOCUMENTS, NEW REVELATIONS, AND A SENATE REPORT THAT TRACED THE ORIGINS OF THOSE METHODS TO HIGH LEVELS IN THE BUSH WHITE HOUSE.

OBAMA REFUSED TO RULE OUT PROSECUTIONS OF THOSE HIGHER-UPS WHO MIGHT HAVE ORDERED TORTURE. CRITICS ON THE LEFT FELT HE WASN'T GOING FAR ENOUGH TO PUNISH THOSE RESPONSIBLE.

SHUT DOWN GUANTANAMO

ON EARTH DAY, OBAMA WAS ABLE TO CHANGE THE TOPIC BY SIGNING THE EDWARD M. KENNEDY SERVICE AMERICA ACT, WHICH WOULD TRIPLE THE NUMBER OF AMERICORPS VOLUNTEERS, TO 250,000, BY 2017.

AS HIS 100TH DAY IN OFFICE NEARED, THE FRESHMAN PRESIDENT WAS STILL RIDING HIGH IN THE POLLS. THERE HAD BEEN SOME DROP-OFF SINCE THE POST-INAUGURAL HONEYMOON, BUT NOT MUCH, AND HE HAD APPROVAL RATINGS OF 69% IN THE ABC/WASHINGTON POST POLL, 65% IN GALLUP, 62% IN FOX NEWS, 63% IN PEW, AND MORE.

63   59   67

Feb 08   Feb 15   Feb 22

HIS FINAL CABINET PICK, KANSAS GOVERNOR KATHLEEN SEBELIUS, WAS CONFIRMED AS HEALTH AND HUMAN SERVICES SECRETARY ON APRIL 28–JUST IN TIME TO DEAL WITH A FEARED SWINE FLU PANDEMIC.

ONE MAJOR SURVEY SHOWED THAT HIS PRESIDENCY HAD ALREADY HELPED ALTER AMERICANS' VIEWS ON RACE, WITH TWO-THIRDS AGREEING THAT RACE RELATIONS ARE GENERALLY GOOD.

APRIL 29, OBAMA'S 100TH DAY, BEGAN WITH A WHITE HOUSE VISIT FROM SENATOR ARLEN SPECTER, WHO HAD JUST SWITCHED PARTY AFFILIATION FROM REPUBLICAN TO DEMOCRATIC.

THE SWITCH WAS POTENTIALLY HUGE FOR THE PRESIDENT, SINCE WHENEVER AL FRANKEN, WHO HAD APPARENTLY WON THE CLOSE RACE IN MINNESOTA, WAS FINALLY SEATED, THE DEMOCRATS WOULD HAVE A FILIBUSTER-PROOF 60-SEAT MAJORITY...

...IF THEY COULD ALL BE PERSUADED TO VOTE TOGETHER.

THE DAY HELD GOOD NEWS AND BAD FOR THE PRESIDENT. CONSUMER STATISTICS SHOWED A SPIKE IN CONFIDENCE AND SPENDING. BUT THE $4 TRILLION BUDGET RESOLUTION HAD TO PASS WITHOUT A SINGLE REPUBLICAN SIGNING ON.

THAT EVENING, HE GAVE HIS THIRD PRIME-TIME PRESS CONFERENCE.

IF YOU COULD TELL ME RIGHT NOW THAT, WHEN I WALKED INTO THIS OFFICE THAT THE BANKS WERE HUMMING, THAT AUTOS WERE SELLING, AND THAT ALL YOU HAD TO WORRY ABOUT WAS IRAQ, AFGHANISTAN, NORTH KOREA, GETTING HEALTH CARE PASSED, FIGURING OUT HOW TO DEAL WITH ENERGY INDEPENDENCE, DEAL WITH IRAN, AND A PANDEMIC FLU, I WOULD TAKE THAT DEAL.

AND—AND THAT'S WHY I'M ALWAYS AMUSED WHEN I HEAR THESE, YOU KNOW, CRITICISMS OF, "OH, YOU KNOW, OBAMA WANTS TO GROW GOVERNMENT." NO. I WOULD LOVE A NICE, LEAN PORTFOLIO TO DEAL WITH, BUT THAT'S NOT THE HAND THAT'S BEEN DEALT US.

AND, YOU KNOW, EVERY GENERATION HAS TO RISE UP TO THE SPECIFIC CHALLENGES THAT CONFRONT THEM. WE HAPPEN TO HAVE GOTTEN A BIG SET OF CHALLENGES, BUT WE'RE NOT THE FIRST GENERATION THAT THAT'S HAPPENED TO. AND I'M CONFIDENT THAT WE ARE GOING TO MEET THESE CHALLENGES JUST LIKE OUR GRANDPARENTS AND FORBEARERS MET THEM BEFORE.

CONGRESS. JULY 4, 1776.

THE CANDIDATE OF CHANGE HAD NOT BEEN ABLE TO CHANGE EVERYTHING. BIPARTISANSHIP REMAINED AN ELUSIVE PRIZE. ALL THE MAJOR PROBLEMS SEEMED INTERRELATED, AND WOULD REQUIRE MORE TIME TO TACKLE.

BUT BARACK OBAMA'S HAD BEEN AN UNLIKELY CANDIDACY, AN UNPREDICTABLE RISE FOR AN INSPIRING INDIVIDUAL. NONE OF IT HAD BEEN EASY, NOT MAKING IT AT HARVARD LAW, ORGANIZING CHICAGO'S SOUTH SIDE, DEFEATING HILLARY CLINTON, OR TAKING ON JOHN McCAIN. HE FOUGHT ONE BATTLE AT A TIME, AND HE PREVAILED.

WATCHING HIM ON THE AMERICAN STAGE, COOL AND COMPOSED NO MATTER WHAT CAME AT HIM, ONE COULD HARDLY HELP THINKING THAT HE WOULD KEEP ON FIGHTING FOR HIS COUNTRY.

MORGAN

HISTORY WOULD JUDGE HIS SUCCESSES AND FAILURES, BUT NO ONE COULD DENY HIS ENERGY, HIS ENTHUSIASM FOR THE JOB, THE NEW OPTIMISM HE BROUGHT TO THE WHITE HOUSE. WASHINGTON—AND THE NATION—HAD ALREADY BEEN CHANGED, JUST BY HIS PRESENCE THERE.

FOR 100 DAYS, AT LEAST, "YES, WE CAN" SEEMED MORE LIKE A PROMISE THAN A SLOGAN. THE PROMISE OF AMERICA, MADE REAL FOR A NEW GENERATION.

Art by J. Scott Campbell
Color by Edgar Delgado

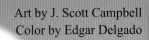
Art by J. Scott Campbell
Color by Edgar Delgado

Art by J. Scott Campbell
Color by Edgar Delgado

SKETCH CARD GALLERY

ARTWORK BY ERIC CANETE

ARTWORK BY JOYCE CHIN

ARTWORK BY CULLY HAMNER

ARTWORK BY LAURA MARTIN

ARTWORK BY LAURA MARTIN

ARTWORK BY LAURA MARTIN

ARTWORK BY BRIAN STELFREEZE

ARTWORK BY BRIAN STELFREEZE

ARTWORK BY BRIAN STELFREEZE

Artwork by Cully Hamner

Artwork by Cully Hamner

Artwork by Cully Hamner

Artwork by Cully Hamner

Artwork by Brian Stelfreeze

Artwork by Brian Stelfreeze

Artwork by Brian Stelfreeze

Artwork by Brian Stelfreeze

Art by Ben Templesmith

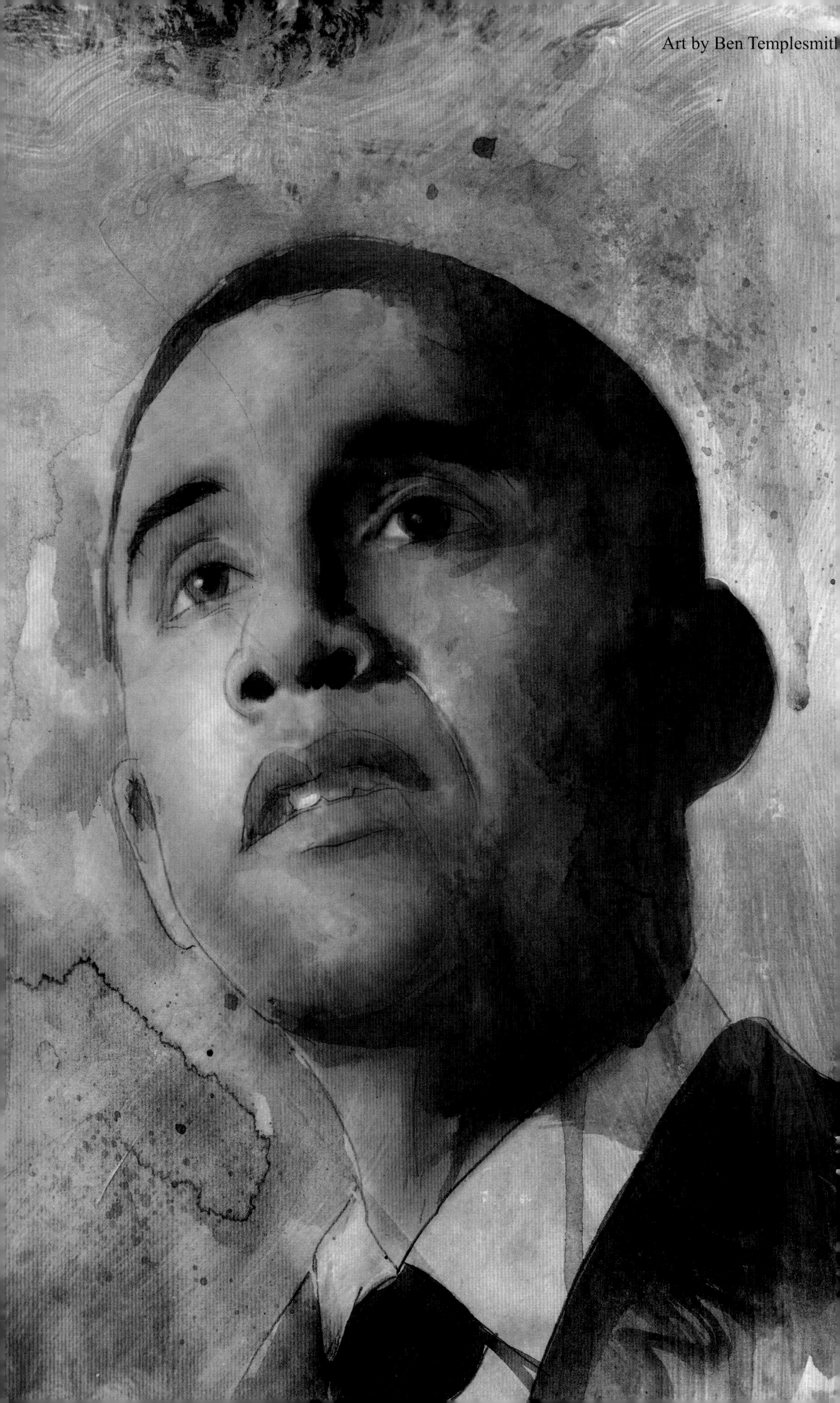